Created to Worship

'*Created to Worship* brings us back to a biblical understanding of what real worship is all about. The reason we exist, why we were created, is to have relationship with and worship the triune God.

The book lays foundations for us about worship, which we would do well to bear in mind as we bring our praise and worship to our Creator. Although our whole lives are worship to God, Bj focuses on our musical and sung worship, especially when we gather together. There are some good challenges for us to consider and some provoking questions for us to answer. However, I pray that this book will help worship leaders, song writers, musicians, and every worshipper not only to have an understanding about worship, but also to find a new release in true worship to the one true God!'

David S Bareham: - Elder Community Church Chafford Hundred, and oversees South Essex Cluster - Relational Mission.

'In a day when myriads of voices seek our attention using all forms of "entertainment", sadly but inevitably, this influence has crept into some Church services, reducing worship to what we sing and how relatable the songs are.

Created to Worship beckons the reader into a meaningful, Christ-centred, holistic relationship with God from which true worship will naturally flow. Bj takes us on a journey through the Scriptures to help us understand what God, rather than man, defines as worship. The book seeks to answer the Who, What, When, Where and How of the reason we exist on Earth – to worship our Creator.

Prepare to have your views challenged, your perspective potentially redefined; your relationship with God invigorated.

I believe Created to Worship is a pivotal addition to the Canon on Worship that exists for today's Church'

Toyin Onabowu: - Choir director, Worship Leader, Author of 'Meditations from Psalms'.

Created to Worship

MAN IS WITHOUT EXCUSE

Bj. Abulude

INSPIRATIONS PUBLISHING

Bj. Abulude
www.bjabulude.com

Created To Worship Bj. Abulude. —1st edition.
ISBN 978-1-9164104-0-4 Inspirations Publishing

Dedicated to the glory of God

'The earth shall be filled with the knowledge of the glory of the Lord as the waters cover the sea.' (Habakkuk 2:14)

Acknowledgements

How could I say Thank You to my Father, Lord and King in a way that would ever begin to be enough? You have been so good to me and my soul knows this very well. I am so grateful You granted me the grace to identify and answer Your call on my life!

> *Most men will proclaim everyone his own goodness: but a faithful man, who can find? (Proverbs 20:6)*

I am grateful for my "faithful man" Temitope for who you are (I wish I could break convention and place an appropriate "emoji" here!) Thank you for being my best friend for as long as I have known you and so much more since... My husband and friend who wants the best for me, believes in me a whole lot more than I believe in myself, and pursues as much as he possibly can, on my behalf...

I am so thankful to God for my indomitable "Triple-O" – Olumide, Oluwafemi and Oluwatobiloba – arrows in the hand of a mighty man; with the Holy Spirit as your teacher and guide, you will all surely remain "more than conquerors in Christ Jesus". Amen.

Thank you, dear Jumoke for helping me to truly "see" Luke 13:6–9.

I am grateful, dear Toyin for your insights and general "hand-holding"...

Thank you to my chief "encourager" Aderoju; you are a joy of many generations!

I am eternally grateful to my parents, Chief D. O. and my late mum, Mrs. M. A. Fadele. You both helped me to develop the love of books from a very young age. Thank you for introducing me to the existence of God, beautiful music and for all the love and laughter!

Contents

Preface

I was apprehended by God from a young age. No, I didn't realise it then, but I have never doubted that God exists. I was an avid reader as a child, so when my dad bought the 10 volume set of 'The Bible Story' by Arthur S Maxwell, I devoured those books. I never imagined that the stories within were anything but true.

Like most people, including those who contest the existence of God, I knew to run to Him whenever I was afraid or confused. I always believed Jesus is real, but I didn't know that I could have a personal, day to day relationship with Him.

I was finally confronted by His Grace and knew I had to choose to live my life for Him. By this time, however, I had also developed a great hindrance. You see, I love music, and love singing. I was always part of my different school choirs, but somehow, I knew that once I dedicated my life to God and His Word, I would have to choose between songs of praise to Him and the clubbing sounds of the mid to late Eighties. No one ever said this to me, but I knew… and this disturbed me greatly. I was disturbed because, prior to this, my experience of 'Christian music' was limited to Hymns, Christmas carols, and traditional Christian music from the radio. It appeared that there was nothing on offer for a young Christian with a love for 'good' music like myself. Interestingly, in a move which taught me something of God's nature and how it is differs from the wiles of the enemy, I was not exposed to the more contemporary style of Christian music until I had made the commitment to fully follow God. Praise God! I was born again by the power of the Holy Spirit and I have been singing to God and for His glory since then.

I became exposed to the music ministries of Integrity Music, Maranatha! Music, The Winans, Brooklyn Tabernacle Choir, Kingdom, Anointed, Amy Grant, Phil Driscoll, to name just a few. These were, to me, seriously gifted musicians, singers and songwriters who had dedicated their gifts to God and were allowing Him to use them for the furtherance of the Gospel and His Kingdom.

I was also blessed to be part of a Church body with an awesome music ministry which took the study of God's word seriously. The music ministry arm of that Church placed equal emphasis on spiritual development as well as the development of musical skills and talents. I was privileged to observe lots of people come to Christ under the conviction of the Holy Spirit after hearing the choir sing; there was no preaching at all. There were also times when the congregation would be so caught up in worship and praise that the Pastor would be unable to preach for the duration of the service.

I came to understand that the Word of God is the carrier of His power and that there was little difference between God's word being spoken or sung. The truth of the gospel is just as easily conveyed in a melody as it is by a preacher. The Spirit of God breathing upon His word is what makes the power of God available; it is the anointing that destroys the yoke. (See Isaiah 10:27)

In the past decade or so, I began to notice disquiet within me, as I became aware of a trend which was making me increasingly uncomfortable.

When I began to listen to Praise and Worship music, the songs were always clear about what they were. They were songs of praise offered to God, and the lyrics reflected this. Of course, there were always other types of songs – songs to edify or 'build up' the Church, songs of repentance and so on, but by and large, the songs of praise were just that. They were dedicated to singing about who God is, what He has done, His character and His Promises. However, I began to notice that a lot of the newer songs were changing focus almost imperceptibly. More and more songs were being presented as songs of Praise or songs for corporate worship, but the subject was no longer about God, but was relating more to how we feel about God, particularly how we feel about Him and what He has done for us. This change as mentioned is subtle, but the negative effects can be far reaching. When we focus on our feelings, we are often tempted to think of ourselves more highly than we should. This, gives rise to the attitude that says "what can God do for me?' rather than, 'why did God place me here? What is my purpose?' Whenever we are overly concerned about how we feel, what we need etc., we become passive Christians who do not understand that God placed us here on earth, for a purpose – His purpose, and that He has already given us access to everything we need to accomplish His plan.

As previously mentioned, the difference is not easy to discern. The challenge I have found is that no matter how well-meaning I am, once my focus is removed from who God is, I am no longer exalting God, but am now in the danger of exalting self instead. Once 'self' takes centre stage, confusion follows close behind. It is always better to concentrate on the greatness of God rather than whatever needs we may be facing. Unfortunately, it appears that more songs are detailing the problems, neglecting the New Covenant, ignoring the indwelling of the Holy Spirit within every born again Christian who receives Him and eventually making the word of God of no effect because of the traditions of men. (Mark 7:13). Nice sounding sentiments are systematically eroding our understanding of the truth of God's word. In the guise of 'humility', rather than acknowledging the good within because the Holy Spirit now lives in us; these songs encourage believers to rehash their shortcomings, passively waiting for God to "come and do" something about the same things He has asked us to deal with. There is a song for example, with such a beautiful melody as to pull on the heartstrings of the most hardened person. My issue with the song, beautiful as it sounds is this. The song says;

'And I, I'm desperate for You, and I, I'm lost without You'

Perhaps it is an appropriate song for an unbelieving person who is just coming to the realisation of the futility of life without God to sing. However, most people who sing it are professing Christians who have ostensibly received the indwelling of the Holy Spirit and have trusted Him to guide and lead them daily. Therefore, while it is true that we would be lost without our Saviour; in light of the dramatic change which occurs at the New Birth, we are no longer 'without Him'. There is no need for us to be looking desperately for Him either, because 'the LORD is near to all who call on Him, to all who call on Him in truth' (Psalm 145: 18).

The most important thing that led me to write this book was the realisation that there are more Christians than I thought, who simply do not know any better, and it also appears that many of those who should know better have forgotten some of the foundational truths they once knew. It is unlikely that this is a deliberate attempt by individuals to kidnap worship and praise, but rather a lack of understanding coupled with the erosion of the truth of God's word from the minds of those who once knew it. Only the enemy has something to gain from this shift. A large number of the younger generation have not even been taught these foundational truths and remain perpetual babes in the Lord.

The meteoric rise of highly skilled worship mega-stars who "perform" in packed out venues complete with cool lighting effects, is causing multitudes to equate gimmicks and effects with the manifest presence of God! (A quick check on some of the most popular Christian YouTube videos is recommended). I do not intend to tar every popular Christian singer, songwriter or musician with the same brush; many do remain uncompromising with the word of God. Instead, I hope to alert everyone to the potential pitfalls of the growing trends in worship and praise music.

I finally realised that God wanted me to do something about what has been causing me this discomfort, so here we are.

I trust God that you, dear reader will be challenged and encouraged by the contents of this book. My earnest hope is that you would take the time to verify any claims made here by going into God's word yourself to see if the thoughts contained herein are truly so.

God bless you richly in Jesus' Name. Amen

We were created for Relationship

This is a mystery – Almighty God, the Creator of the Universe, according to the scriptures; 'chose us in Him *BEFORE* the foundation of the world...' (Ephesians 1:4). God planned for our existence before He created the Universe.

> *'The heaven, even the heavens, are the LORD'S: but the earth hath He given to the children of men.' (Psalm 115:16)*

These verses, along with other supporting passages in the Bible, underscore the fact that while the Almighty God made mankind for Himself, He formed the Earth and everything within it for us. The reason for this is explained in Acts 17:26–28:

> *'And He made from one man every nation of mankind to live on all the face of the earth, having determined allotted periods and the boundaries of their dwelling place that they should seek God, and perhaps feel their way toward Him and find Him. Yet He is actually not far from each one of us, for "In Him we live and move and have our being'; as even some of your own poets have said, 'for we are indeed His offspring."'(Acts 17: 26–28 ESV)*

God created mankind so that He may have fellowship with us, but the fellowship He desires is dependent on our will. The twenty-seventh verse of Acts 17 above reveals His desire that we seek and ultimately find Him, though it must be our own choice. Although He is near to us (*He is not actually far from us*), the choice is given to man to seek God or try to live independently of Him. As a result of this opportunity to choose, a vast number of people continue to try to live without even acknowledging the existence of the Creator, though, in reality, we cannot live completely without Him. It is in Him that we live and move and have our being!

God began His work of creation, by fashioning the environment in which man would live. He did this in such a way that everything that the first man and every subsequent human being would ever require to sustain life on the earth was already available, long before that need was ever identified!

The eternal Creator 'spoke' everything (including mankind) in this physical realm into existence. We understand from the Bible that before He made man from the dust of the earth, He ***said:***

> *'...Let us make man in our image, after our likeness: and let them have dominion over the fish of the sea, and over the fowl of the air, and over the cattle, and over all the earth, and over every creeping thing that creepeth upon the earth. So God created man in His own image, in the image of God created He him; male and female created He them.' (Genesis 1:26, 27)*

In the next chapter, we see that God not only declared His intention to create man, but that '...the Lord God formed man of the dust of the ground and breathed into his nostrils the breath of life; and man became a living soul' (Genesis 2:7).

Man was made in the image and likeness of God, meaning that He intended that we would be like Him! He breathed into man the breath of life, separating man from everything else He had created. In the first man, Adam, God placed a part of Himself; 'He breathed into his nostrils' and he became a living soul.

As a result of the fall of Adam and his wife Eve, the close connection which God originally intended to have with mankind was broken.

Evidence of the close relationship Adam and his wife enjoyed with the Almighty God is found as we read: '...they heard the voice of the Lord walking in the garden in the cool of the day' (Genesis 3:8). They knew God enough to recognise His voice and were expecting to see and be seen by Him. They would not have felt the need to hide from His presence otherwise. Besides, God had previously brought all the animals He had created before Adam to see what he would call them (Genesis 3:19).

To restore (at least partially at this time) God's relationship with mankind, a sacrifice had to be made. Our compassionate Father killed an animal so He could make a coat of skins for Adam and Eve. He did this so they would no longer feel the need to hide from His presence, naked and ashamed. This was the first shedding of blood, the first sacrifice. (Genesis 3:21).

We must remember that there was a penalty for sin. The instruction given to Adam was undeniable; '...for in the day that you eat of it, you shall surely die' (Genesis 2:17b). That first sacrifice meant that the animal took on (albeit temporarily) the penalty for man's sin. The law of God is clear: '...without the shedding of blood, there is no forgiveness of sins' (Hebrews 9:22, Leviticus 17:11).

God provided a substitute to take on the punishment that the sinner deserved, and killed an animal so that Adam and Eve would live. Blessed is our God who made a new and living way for us to come into His presence – by the blood of The Lamb! Hallelujah!

The direct and easy relationship between man and his God was almost irrevocably damaged as a result of that single act of disobedience! Adam (Mankind), created for fellowship, created to worship the Almighty God, was suddenly presented with a myriad of options and distractions, because his eyes were now opened. The break in fellowship also meant Adam felt he could no longer approach God boldly as before; choosing to hide from His presence instead!

Interestingly, because mankind was created to relate with, fellowship with and worship the Almighty Creator; many still try to find God, though most are not able to articulate what it is they seek. Even to this day, regardless of the opportunities, the increase of knowledge, the "age of enlightenment" and all the distractions we are faced with, we surely must concede that everyone has at least one object of worship in their lives. This is the same for those who have or profess faith in a deity and those who do not. There is a need to hold something or someone in greater esteem than all others!

This need to worship something or someone (including one's self, as narcissists are claimed to do), appears to be an innate need in the life of every human being. If we go along with this premise, we are able to easily identify those things which take a central or top position in our lives and admit that these things have become idols which we have consciously or otherwise replaced God with.

> *'...who changed the truth of God into a lie, and worshipped and served the creature more than the Creator, who is blessed forever. Amen.' (Romans 1:25).*

Nevertheless, in His mercy, God still allows us to identify our need for Him, particularly when we come to the end of our abilities and discover that we have more questions than answers outside of Him. We are drawn to Him and finally acknowledge the existence of the Greater One!

Once we discover and accept His claim on our lives, the questions arise: How do I relate to the Almighty God? I know that He created the heavens and the earth. He fashioned the

worlds and those who live in it; God formed man for His pleasure – but how do I please God? How do I relate to Him?
We will be exploring these and other questions as they pertain in particular to our Worship, and in doing so, we should consider this: God, who took the time to not only bring us into being, but also thought of making a comfortable environment in which we can thrive, surely deserves something from us in return.
If we follow the preceding questions to their logical conclusion, we discover that not only does God deserve our worship, but that we *need* to worship Him. We also find out that there is evidence in the scriptures, confirmed in what we can see in the world around us, which prove that refusing to worship God is not a viable option! In the first chapter of the book of Romans, we see some of the consequences of choosing *not* to honour Him as God; choosing not to worship God. We shall be looking at this in some detail a little later.
As we become convinced that we were indeed, created to worship, honour and serve God; and we acknowledge that we do not belong to ourselves; the next step would be for us to acknowledge that there is a prescribed method for our worship. We cannot presume to make things up according to our own whims and designs and should appreciate the requirement for us to search out this prescription from the word of God. The following verse details this prescription:

> *'God is a Spirit; and they that worship Him MUST worship Him in spirit and in truth' (John 4:24 – emphasis mine).*

This is an absolute statement with no room for discussion. Jesus said in essence; have you chosen to worship God? Then you must worship Him in spirit and in truth.

- Who then is a worshipper? What does it mean for us to worship God? Is our worship encapsulated in singing songs about God or to Him? Are there some other dimensions to our worship?

- What does our worship look like in the 21st Century? Should it be any different in format from what is revealed in the scriptures to be relevant to our generation? Do we even know what exactly is revealed in the scriptures?
- Should our worship be relevant and inclusive to engage the younger generations or to draw the hearts of those yet to receive God's salvation?
- If so, how do we achieve this, or if not, why not?

These and other related questions are the focus of this book, to encourage every believer in Christ into a better understanding of something evidently dear to our Heavenly Father's heart. I strongly believe that our worship encapsulates the reason we exist – that this is the reason for which you and I were created!

In addition to the life of the individual worshipper, we shall also explore our 21st Century congregational worship, with particular reference to worship leading, writing songs for worship as well as the role of the worship team within our congregations.

CHAPTER 1

What is He worth?

The human race has no excuse for not glorifying the Creator as God and worshipping Him for who He is.

> *'For the wrath of God is revealed from heaven against all ungodliness and unrighteousness of men, who by their unrighteousness suppress the truth. For what can be known about God is plain to them because God has shown it to them. For His invisible attributes, namely, His eternal power and divine nature have been clearly perceived, ever since the creation of the world, in the things that have been made. So they are without excuse. For although they knew God, they did not honour him as God or give thanks to him, but they became futile in their thinking, and their foolish hearts were darkened.' (Romans 1:18–21 ESV).*

A God Spot?

The preceding Bible verses affirm that God designed mankind with the ability to recognise Him through the things He made. This means that anyone who chooses not to honour God for whom He is does not have an excuse. What can be known about God is clear; all anyone needs to do is just look around at those things He created.

A popular statement espoused by a good number of evangelists says; within every human being is an otherwise empty portion that can only be filled by God Himself! Indeed, songwriters Christopher Dwight Harris and Denise Yvonne Walls in their song aptly titled "God Spot"[1] describe this as the part of man which nothing or no one else could ever satisfactorily fill. This assertion, though often vehemently opposed by those who deny God's existence, is nonetheless proven by the way those same people choose to live their lives!

Interestingly, even scientists and psychologists have waded into this debate, seeking to either confirm or downplay the existence of this 'God Spot' within human beings. Some argue that an actual physical portion of the brain controls religious belief, while others are convinced no particular area of the brain holds a God spot; instead, several parts of the brain work together in complex combinations.

Whichever side of the debate we choose to stand on, it is difficult to deny the fact that human beings seem never to be satisfied, but are always striving for more; notwithstanding what they have already attained or achieved!

Even a brief glance into the lives of those who appear to "have everything" reveals an apparent dissatisfaction which is often displayed in the insatiable quest for knowledge, power, and admiration. This is quite apart from the self-destructive vices played out in so many of those lives! The conclusion of the matter, which only those who have received the grace of God into their lives can ever come to accept, is that the man who chooses not to accept nor worship God as the Creator is only trading the glory of God Almighty for an image, a mirage, a strong delusion (Romans 1:18–32). A disastrously imbalanced trade! The truth, whether we choose to acknowledge it or not, is that you and I were created by the Supreme being – Almighty

---

[1] God Spot: Songwriters Christopher Dwight Harris/ Denise Yvonne Walls. Performed by Anointed Released 1999.

God Himself so that He may relate with us. This relationship has the potential to develop into deep levels of intimacy and communion, which achieves the ultimate goal for the creation of mankind. In relating with God, we encounter His holiness and are awed by Him. Expressing this awe leads us to worship Him; seeking to serve Him with everything we are and have, recognising that we do not belong to ourselves but to God!

As it becomes evident that human beings were created to worship, for those who accept Adonai as Creator, God and King; the next question might be: what is worship?

Worship is defined in several ways; however, in Webster's 1828 dictionary, the transitive verb 'worship' is defined as 'to adore; to pay divine honours to; to reverence with supreme respect and veneration.'

When we acknowledge our Everlasting Father as God Almighty, it becomes paramount that He receives the honour He deserves from us. The contemporary English word 'worship' comes from the old English word 'weorthscipe' which is defined as 'the acknowledgement of worth'.

What value do we place on God? How highly do we esteem Him? The sense of value and worth we place on God will determine how we live our lives as worshippers.

If we truly desire to honour God, we would instinctively want to obey Him. Our desire to obey brings us to the realisation that first, we must know what He commands. If we desire a close relationship with someone else, we would at the very least find out what the other person likes or dislikes. We may also want to identify those things they are indifferent to, and what they absolutely abhor! This is much the same with developing our relationship with our Heavenly Father. The scriptures declare:

> *'But without faith it is impossible to please Him: for he that cometh to God must believe that He is, and that He is a rewarder of them that diligently seek Him.' (Hebrews 11:6).*

This contradicts the actions of those atheists or agnostics who pray when faced with contrary circumstances and then rail at the God whose existence they had always denied when things do not turn out as they had hoped. Acknowledging that God *IS* real is absolutely fundamental to seeking, finding, and eventually developing a close relationship with Him. Moreover, we do not develop a true and lasting relationship with someone else by using a "hit and miss" approach. To make a marriage last, for instance, a fair amount of work is required. If what we are hoping to gain is to be worthwhile in the long run, we must be ready to pay the price.

> *'I beseech you, therefore, brethren, by the mercies of God, that you present your bodies a living sacrifice, holy, acceptable to God, which is your reasonable service'. (Romans 12:1 NKJV)*

The minimum requirement for every true Christian who seeks to be a worshiper is to dedicate our entire lives to God. Practically speaking, this means that there is no part of our existence that we would knowingly keep from Him.

Everyone who wishes to live a life of worship must determine what God is worth to them. How far would I go for Him? Why would I go that far? What am I willing to give up; to sacrifice, to help me to preserve my relationship with Him?

In the New Covenant, nothing outside each of us can sever our relationship with God. There is no external force powerful enough to separate us from God's love! This is the true sense of Romans 8:38–39 which declares:

> *'For I am sure that neither death nor life, nor angels nor rulers, nor things present nor things to come, nor powers, nor height nor depth, nor anything else in all creation, will be able to separate us from the love of God in Christ Jesus our Lord.' (ESV)*

God has repeatedly promised that nothing can separate us from His love. He will never leave us nor forsake us – but we can forsake Him and choose to go our own way. The preservation of our relationship with God is not up to Him as some may think. It is up to us to draw nigh unto Him and He has promised that He, in turn, will draw nigh unto us (see James 4:8).

We must admit the futility of an existence without God, because He created us for His pleasure, and as a function of His will:

'Thou art worthy, O Lord, to receive glory and honour and power: for thou hast created all things, and for thy pleasure they are and were created.' (Revelation 4:11)

We should also understand that God does not *need* us to worship Him; instead, we need Him because our existence depends on His will, His plan, and His design. He chose to create us; we had no say in the matter!

> *'The God who made the world and everything in it, being Lord of heaven and earth, does not live in temples made by man, nor is He served by human hands, as though He needed anything, since He Himself gives to all mankind life and breath and everything' (Acts 17:24–25 ESV)*

There is a cost

Our Lord Jesus said, 'If any man would come after Me, let him deny himself, and take up his cross and follow Me' (Matthew 16:24, Luke 9:23). This invitation alerts us to the fact that there is a cost to serving God. This cost involves living a life that belongs solely to Him. To deny myself is to acknowledge that I am effectively owned by Him; we have sold our will to God and are ready to obey His command, regardless of any contrary thoughts or ideas we may have.

Jesus, speaking about the cost of following Him, said:

> *'If anyone comes to Me and does not hate his father and mother, wife and children, brothers and sisters, yes, and his*

> *own life also, he cannot be My disciple. And whoever does not bear his cross and come after Me cannot be My disciple. For which of you, intending to build a tower, does not sit down first and count the cost, whether he has enough to finish it?' (Luke 14:26–28 NKJV)*

Everyone who decides to be a worshipper (and therefore a disciple or a disciplined follower) of the Most High must take a moment to count the cost! Though salvation is a free gift, discipleship is something we have to work at consciously and consistently. This is why Philippians 2:12 admonishes us to work out our own salvation with fear and trembling. The entire Kingdom of heaven is likened to a merchant looking for fine pearls, who, on discovering one pearl of great value, *went and sold everything he had,* to purchase it (Matthew 13:45–46).

Once again, I ask: what is He worth to you? What price is too great for you to pay to fully follow Him? These are questions we must ask ourselves, particularly as the Day of the Lord (the end of this world as we know it; the return of our Lord Jesus Christ as He promised) approaches. The times and seasons we are in are getting more and more perilous, particularly for those who profess faith in Christ alone. The insidious nature of the times we live in today is such that if we are not vigilant, it is surprisingly easy to fall into the enemy's trap. There are thorns and thistles, the cares of this world and the deceitfulness of riches, all standing at the ready to choke everything we know of God from us (Matthew 13:22). This is why it is vital, for our wellbeing, to keep our eyes fixed upon God and His word.

So, what can I do, how can I show God that I hold Him alone in the highest regard in my life? How do I know, without a doubt, that I truly adore Him as my Father, my King, my God? How do I live completely sold-out to Him? The prophet Habakkuk has an unusual, powerful insight here:

> *'Although the fig tree shall not blossom, neither shall fruit be in the vines; the labour of the olive shall fail, and the fields*

> *shall yield no meat; the flock shall be cut off from the fold, and there shall be no herd in the stalls: Yet I will rejoice in the LORD, I will joy in the God of my salvation.' (Habakkuk 3:17, 18)*

This is someone who evidently has chosen to worship God in spite of personal circumstances. He asserts: *although nothing appears to be working right for me, I choose to rejoice in God my Maker.* That we are alive is more than enough reason to fix our gaze on Him in adoration and praise! We should resist the temptation to approach God with the 'what can He give to me' attitude and focus on what we can and should consistently do to ensure that we are in constant communication with Him.

Neglecting the importance of staying in communication with God was at the root of the children of Israel's continuous backsliding. The scriptures declare: 'He made known His ways unto Moses, His acts unto the children of Israel' (Psalm 103:7). The result of this distinction between the ways and acts of God is made clearer in Psalm 78:11; 'They forgot His works and the wonders that He had shown them.' This highlights the fact that the children of Israel did not remember the mighty deeds God had performed on their behalf! It is almost mind-blowing to consider that those who crossed the Red Sea by walking on dry land could ever forget how great God is! Yet, they did forget, and murmured against Him soon afterwards. Does this not echo the lives of countless Christians today; those who ignore how good God has been to them as they choose to fixate on a specific problem or desire?

We must seek to know God's ways, not His acts alone! This is what differentiates us from those who do not know Him.

Note that the entire nation of Israel had similar access to the knowledge of God's ways in addition to His acts. Indeed, His acts were, and are still easily recognised by those who were not part of the covenant. Interestingly, James 2:19 brings a new perspective into this matter: 'you believe that there is one God.

You do well. Even the demons believe; and tremble!' A Christian who merely believes in God has done no more than demons have. As a matter of fact, the demons may have done more – they tremble as a result of the information they possess. Demons know that God exists, so they cower in fear! In contrast, a disproportionately large percentage of those who profess Christianity do not appear to fear God in the least!

Compare the prophet Habakkuk's response above to that of numerous professing Christians today, who would say, for instance, 'I asked God for X, Y, Z; I have been waiting for so long for His answer but He didn't give it to me, so I am angry with Him. I am no longer interested in following Him'. The situation described here may be hypothetical, but similar thinking is the motivation behind the actions of a large number of people who once professed faith in Jesus, but allowed themselves to be deceived and ultimately cheated of an eternally rewarding relationship with Him.

Multitudes have been deceived into walking out on the faith they once knew, due to some disappointment they experienced or perhaps acts of hypocrisy they uncovered. Interestingly, according to a poll of nearly 300,000 self-professed atheists, 35% claim to have come from broadly Christian backgrounds, while an additional 29% claim they were originally Catholics.[2]

We would do well to remember the patriarch Abraham who is often referred to as the "father of faith". Abraham counted obedience to God worth more than his most prized possession, his son Isaac, as he lay Isaac down to be sacrificed in complete obedience to God's command!

This incredible account of one man's faith in God does beg the question; "why would God ask Abraham to do this?" Why would He ask Abraham to give up his most prized possession in

---

[2] (http://www.atheistcensus.com)

this way? This is a point to ponder; as it is a test (maybe not in such a dramatic manner) we all must pass in our walk with God. We can surmise that this is so because He has revealed Himself to be a jealous God. He must take first place in our lives or He has no place at all! Anything else that takes that premier place, however legitimate, becomes an idol! This is a good time to reflect on your individual situation; what do you value the most in your life? In what order do you prioritise that thing? Do you value anything more than your relationship with God?

Our newly created spirits, (for the born-again believer in Christ Jesus) are drawn almost automatically towards God, and, as we learn to yield to the longing of our spirits rather than the demands of our flesh, we become true worshippers who count no cost too great for the joy of knowing and serving the One who created us.

POINTS TO PONDER

---

1. Do you believe that there is a 'God spot' in every human being? If you are a Christian, think back on the time just before you gave your heart to Christ; can you with hindsight see how you were led to God?
2. What value, if any do you place upon your relationship with God. Are you content to leave it at just having accepted Jesus Christ as your Lord and Saviour? Or perhaps, you have come to the realisation that you need to develop a closer walk with Him. Whose responsibility do you think it is to foster that relationship? Yours or God's?

3. Is there a cost to following Jesus? Can you think of any specific thing you have done or decided to do in order to foster a closer relationship with God? Is there anything you have given up?
4. What do you think this means to you; the idea that nothing external can separate you from God's love?

CHAPTER 2

What is Praise, what is Worship?

'Praise ye the LORD. Praise God in His sanctuary: praise Him in the firmament of His power. Praise Him for His mighty acts: praise Him according to His excellent greatness. Praise Him with the sound of the trumpet: praise Him with the psaltery and harp. Praise Him with the timbrel and dance: praise Him with stringed instruments and organs. Praise Him upon the loud cymbals: praise Him upon the high-sounding cymbals. Let everything that hath breath praise the LORD. Praise ye the LORD'. (Psalm: 150).

In the book of Psalms, again and again, we see the command to 'Praise the Lord'. Note that this is always a command rather than a mere suggestion! What then does it mean to praise the Lord; does this differ from worshipping the Lord? What, if any, are these differences?

What is Praise?

There are several dictionary definitions of praise; including – to commend, to applaud; to express approbation or approval of something or someone. Praise is also defined as, 'To extol (to proclaim the glory of someone or something) in words or song;

to magnify, to glorify on account of perfections or excellent works'. (Webster 1828).

We also praise by giving honour to; displaying the excellence of something or someone; 'All Thy works shall praise Ye O Lord!' (Psalm 145)

Several Hebrew words and phrases in the Bible are translated as Praise in the English Language. It is, therefore, a good exercise for the Christian to study all these forms of praise, as they are ways to praise God as revealed in the scriptures:

Yadah: This word comes from a root word in Hebrew which means "to throw", or "the extended hand"; "to throw out the extended hand". Therefore, to *"yadah"* God means to worship Him with hands lifted up. This form of praise was first revealed in Genesis 29:35 when Leah named her last-born son, Judah; saying 'Now will I praise the LORD'.

Consider this for a moment; have you ever been part of, seen videos or even pictures of a pop concert where practically every person present has their arms raised up high? The next time you or those around you experience this phenomenon, take some time to think about what you (or the people you are observing) are doing. Who is being worshipped at that point in time? Is it the pop star or the musicians? Is God being worshipped here???

Towdah: The word *Towdah* is similar to the first word *Yadah* and also means an extension of the hand, with palms raised up high, thanking God with adoration and often in a sacrifice of praise. For example, in Psalm 147:7 – 'Sing unto the LORD with thanksgiving; sing praise upon the harp unto our God'. The word rendered thanksgiving here is the word "Towdah" in Hebrew.

Halal: Is a verb and the root of the word Hallelujah. This word means - to shine, and also means to make a show; to boast, be clamorous and foolish; to rave! Therefore, when we shout Hallelujah; we are in essence saying, "we make our boast in You, Lord!" Psalm 44:8 says: 'In God we *boast* all day long and praise Your Name forever'. The word translated "boast" here, is the word *Halal.*

Barak: To kneel or bow before God. This means to "bless" God as an act of adoration. The word Barak is translated "bless" numerous times in scriptures as in Psalm 34:1 – 'I will *bless* the LORD at all times: His praise shall continually be in my mouth.'

Shabach: To address in a loud tone, to shout, to give loud adoration. This word gives a sense of praising God without being self-conscious. (Psalm 117:1 – 'O praise the LORD, all ye nations: *praise* Him all ye people'. In this verse, the first word rendered "praise" is the word *Halal* while the second italicised word is *Shabach.*

Zamar: This Hebrew word means to sing with instruments; to touch the strings; making music accompanied by the voice, as mentioned in Psalm 92:1; 'It is a good thing to give thanks unto the LORD and to sing *praises* unto Thy Name, O most High'. Psalm 150 also speaks extensively of praising God by singing and playing instruments.

Tehillah: A hymn of praise. Tehillah often refers to singing an unprepared, unrehearsed song (which is sometimes known as the spontaneous song) from a melody within your heart. 'I will bless the Lord at all times, His *praise* (Tehillah) shall continually be in my mouth.' (Psalm 34:1). Psalm 22:3; which speaks of God inhabiting the praises of Israel, the word "praises" is translated from the Hebrew word Tehillah. This is not a stretch then, to conclude that God chooses to inhabit those praises that originate directly from our hearts!

The definitions of the preceding most common Hebrew words translated "praise" illustrate the fact that our praise is visual, visible, and external. Our praise can, and should be seen and heard, even from a distance! This indisputable fact reveals the error of those who choose to sit quietly and contemplatively, confidently thinking, "I am praising God in my own way"! If we were truly honest with ourselves, we would admit that if there were some dignitary or famous pop star standing in front of us, we would instantly adopt the proper protocols for being in their presence. When the Queen of England enters a room, everyone in that room is expected to stand. Seriously, consider the way crowds of fans go berserk when a major pop star appears on stage or even the obsession of the "fan boys and fan girls" who compulsively follow the subject of their adoration. Why are we eager to afford mere mortals high levels of respect, even adulation, yet often remain dispassionate when "welcoming" the manifest presence of the King of kings and Lord of lords**?**

The call to praise God is a command, not a suggestion. The Bible is replete with this **command** because God is worthy of our praise. When some Pharisees asked Jesus to rebuke His disciples who were praising Him '...with a loud voice for all the mighty works they had seen', He told those Pharisees that if the praise stopped, the stones 'would immediately cry out' (see Luke 19: 37–40).

When we praise God, we declare His praises, show forth His praise, we are clamorously foolish, we bow prostrate before Him, tell of all His wondrous works, we sing to Him, we sing about Him, we dance before Him – a lot of activity is involved in truly praising God... What we absolutely do not do, is stay silent and immobile!

Here then lies the subtle difference between "Worship" and "Praise". Praise can be viewed as a subset of worship because, as we discovered earlier, worship is ascribing worth to God. Our praise ascribes worth to God because praise is preoccupied with "making much ado" about Him. Some have described praise as being "horizontal" in the sense that when we praise God, we often are not necessarily declaring our praises *to* Him, rather, we tell others about what He has done or who He has revealed Himself to be. "Worship" however, is deemed to be "vertical" inasmuch as it is always directed to God Himself.

The postures we adopt when offering praises to God differ from those we use when we are in a time of deep adoration and worship. When we are making a great deal of noise, shouting, clapping and dancing, the loud sound of rejoicing would make it much more difficult to sense the "still small voice" of the Holy Spirit. However, when we are in an attitude of reverential worship, with the attendant positions of kneeling or bowing before our God and King in awe and wonder, or in total adoration, it is easier to quiet our hearts and minds in order to listen to, and respond to, the voice of the Spirit.

We can conclude, therefore, that praise is *NOT* just what we do before we worship. Our praises are an integral part of worship to God. We do not differentiate praise from worship by saying; praise is the fast songs, while worship is the slower songs either. We must also understand that "praise and worship" in the context of a Church service do not represent a kind of warm-up act before the Word is brought to the assembly. As we shall see later, our worship, our praise, the bringing of the word or preaching, and ultimately, the way we live our lives, are all fundamental parts of our worship; our service to our great God.

What is Worship?

> *'But the hour cometh, and now is, when the true worshippers shall worship the Father in spirit and in truth: for the Father seeketh such to worship Him. God is a Spirit: and they that worship Him must worship Him in spirit and in truth.' (John 4: 23, 24).*

Jesus was speaking here with a woman from Samaria and a few things immediately become evident from His entire conversation with her:

- Our worship is no longer dependent upon being at a specific location. (The Jews had to go to Jerusalem – or at least face the direction of Jerusalem to worship).

- We need to know **who** we worship. It is quite possible to think we are worshipping the Almighty God, though we have sadly replaced Him with an idol of our own making.
- There are those who are called "true worshippers". What makes them true worshippers is the fact that they worship the Father in spirit and in truth; and the Father actively ***seeks*** for such people to worship Him.

Our worship is no longer dependent on a specific physical location:

The Bible, in 2 Corinthians 6:16, tells us that we are the temple of God, and that the Spirit of God lives in us, citing Leviticus 26:12. Here, God says: 'I will make my dwelling among them, and walk in them; and I will be their God, and they shall be my people'. This is our firm assurance that God is with us wherever we are – we carry His presence! Praise God, because of the New Covenant, we are able to not only boldly approach the Creator of the Universe, but also have His presence with us at all times. Hallelujah!

Who or what do you worship?

In saying to the Samaritan woman: 'you worship you know not what', Jesus emphasises the importance of knowing who or what the object of our worship is. As we previously established, within every human being is a need to worship something or someone; and while even creation, the heavens declare the glory of God and the skies above show His handiwork (Psalm 19:1); there are those who still refuse to honour God as Creator. The only way to know for sure that we worship the God who created the heavens and the earth is to know Him through His revealed Word.

If we do not take the time and effort to know Him through His Word, we run the risk of finding ourselves sadly worshipping some other god we have created for ourselves – a figment of our own imaginations. This is the crux of why countless fall into error. They begin to create a god in their imaginations which differs completely from Almighty God. This is what happened, for instance, when the Jews saw the Messiah whom they had been waiting for, for so long. They did not accept Jesus as Messiah because He differed considerably from what they had come to expect. They were expecting a strong military ruler who would save them from the oppression of Rome and He showed up as a baby in a manger!

In the 21st Century, vast numbers of people are being deceived as more Christian leaders, taking their "followers" with them, bow to the pressures of political correctness and sentiments. Therefore, the ancient landmarks revealed in the scriptures are no longer considered relevant. Large numbers are then drawn away to a Universalist, hedonistic "gospel" which bears little resemblance to the Good News that Jesus proclaimed while He walked the Earth. Some people continue to suggest that our understanding of the scriptures should be adjusted to the fact that we now live in the twenty-first century. One of the results is that a plethora of updates and upgrades to Bible versions are being created in order to present something cool, fresh and relevant.

We have got to settle this within ourselves once and for all: God does not change! God will not change! If He were to change even by an iota, the universe will implode. This may sound like a gross exaggeration until we begin to consider the full consequences of a changeable God. The Bible tells us that He upholds *ALL* things by the Word of His power. If He were to yield and go back on His Word concerning something or the other, what would happen to those things He is holding up by His Word?

> *'For they deliberately overlook this fact, that the heavens existed long ago, and the earth was formed out of water and through water by the word of God, and that by means of these, the world that then existed was deluged with water and perished. But by the same word the heavens and earth that now exist are stored up for fire, being kept until the Day of Judgment and destruction of the ungodly.' (2 Peter 3:5-7 ESV)*

God's word is what is keeping the Universe together right now; until the time He has appointed, when it will be destroyed by fire, and He will create a New Heaven and a New Earth.
In Genesis 9:11 for instance, God promised (gave His word); '...I will establish My covenant with you; neither shall all flesh be cut off any more by the waters of a flood; neither shall there be any more a flood to destroy the earth.' What if His word could change? I think it is safe to say those catastrophic consequences are better imagined than experienced. Praise God that He does not change! Again, let us consider this: Jesus said, 'Not everyone that saith unto me, Lord, Lord, shall enter into the kingdom of heaven; but he that doeth the will of my Father which is in heaven' (Matthew 7:21). How can this profound statement be understood in any other way? If we do not do the Father's will; no matter how much we have proclaimed the gospel, we cannot enter into the kingdom of heaven. While this is not the intended message of this book, we should accept that we need a God that does not change, (as He revealed Himself to us through the Scriptures), rather than succumb to the deception pervading society today. The vocal liberal twenty-first century voices are bent on creating a universal "god" whom they try to present as the Almighty God. The true child of God, the true worshipper and disciple of Jesus Christ, must ensure they know whom they worship. Remember the grave warning Jesus gave in Matthew 24:24, '...there shall arise false christs and false

prophets, and shall shew great signs and wonders; insomuch that, if it were possible, *they shall deceive the very elect.*'

Multitudes have been deceived in this way, including those who did not accept the Messiah when He walked the Earth. As a result, some Jews are still looking forward to the coming of the Messiah today, though He has already come in the flesh. (See John 1:11 – 'He came unto His own, and His own received Him not'). They did not recognise Him because He did not conform to their image of the Messiah. This is in spite of the fact that Jesus' first coming fulfilled all the prophecy about the Messiah in the scriptures!

True Worship – In spirit and in truth:

To attempt to worship without the truth is the same as idolatry. This is because, without the truth, you are NOT worshipping the Almighty. Worshipping without your spirit's involvement is dead. Without your spirit's involvement, you simply are not worshipping the living God because your heart, the essence of who you are, is literally not in it.

In John 4:24, we are told '...God is a Spirit, and those who would worship Him MUST worship Him in spirit and in truth.'

First, we should note the differences between God the Spirit and the spirit of man in the preceding verse.

There is a foundational truth which must be embraced and understood by every born-again Christian; that is, those who have been born of the Holy Spirit. Everyone who would live in the fullness of the "Abundant life" (John 10:10) that Jesus Christ purchased and freely gives to us must know this: As **God is Spirit,** so **man IS spirit.** Man is essentially a spirit who possesses a soul and lives in a body.

> *'Now may the God of peace Himself sanctify you completely, and may your whole spirit and soul and body be kept*

blameless at the coming of our Lord Jesus Christ.' (1 Thessalonians 5:23 ESV)

Some Bible scholars have explored this further and found that the scriptures speak of our salvation in three separate tenses:

- We have been saved (2 Timothy 1:9 – past tense),
- We are being saved (1 Corinthians 1:18; Philippians 2: 12–13; – present continuous tense), and
- We shall be saved! (Romans 5:9–10, — future tense).

Though a thorough exposition of this truth is not within the scope of this book, we should concede that the only part of us that truly communicates with God is our spirit – the new creature in Christ (2 Corinthians 5:17). This is the part of the born-again Christian that is "fully saved" right now; the completely new creation in Christ Jesus!

Therefore, no one who is yet to receive the saving grace of God through the gift of His Son Jesus; no one who is yet to be born-again can truly worship Him as God.

To worship God, we must engage our spirit, though both our soul and body obviously participate. In 1 Corinthians 14:2, we are given more insight into the tripartite (consisting of three parts) nature of man; 'For he who speaks in a tongue does not speak to men but to God, for no one understands him; however, ***in the spirit*** he speaks mysteries.' (NKJV)

We know that our body is not saved yet but will be saved at the return of our Lord in glory, when we are changed from mortal into immortality (1 Corinthians 15:52, 53). Nevertheless, we must realise that the transformation of the soul part of man is up to him. A man's soul is described as the part of him which contains or controls his will, mind, character and emotions. Romans 12:2 says that we should 'be transformed by the renewal of your minds'.

Worship in Truth:

In much the same way as we worship in spirit, we must also worship God in truth. This statement may appear ambiguous until we realise that:

Jesus is – The way, the TRUTH and the life; no one comes to the Father except through Him; (John 14:6 – emphasis mine).

We are sanctified by the TRUTH; His Word is TRUTH (John 17:17 – emphasis mine)

Jesus is the Word of God that became flesh and dwelt amongst us. Jesus IS God (John 1:1 – 'In the beginning was the Word, and the Word was with God, and the Word was God').

Worship in truth involves worshipping God in accordance with His revealed Word, rather than our sentiments, emotions, wishes or aspirations. His revealed word here is to emphasise the fact that God is the only One who, by His Spirit, can interpret His written word. (See 2 Peter 1:20)

Truth here is concerned with God's true nature revealed in the scriptures rather than the sincerity of the person worshipping, after all, to be sincerely wrong is still wrong.

God's word is not something we decipher by intellectual study only; we need the illumination the Holy Spirit alone can give. It is small wonder then, that untold multitudes over the course of history have committed countless atrocities in the name of "God" because they have misinterpreted the scriptures.

At the other end of the spectrum are those who choose to interpret the scriptures in such a way as to make it say what they want it to say.

When, for instance, we seek to claim God's promises as seen in the scriptures without first finding out what the conditions attached to those promises are, we are setting ourselves up for a fall. The salvation that God provides is completely free, but all His promises are conditional. Some have declared for example; because God is love, therefore there can be no judgement for my disobedience... So they depend on His forgiveness while they remain unrepentant. Unfortunately, too many in the Body of Christ do not seem to fully grasp this truth yet, and it shows in the way they live their lives. A lot of professing Christians continue to live far beneath the reality of those '...exceeding great and precious promises through which we are meant to be partakers of God's divine nature.' (2 Peter 1:4)

It is sad to acknowledge that God's people are still being 'destroyed for the lack of knowledge'. This is a lack of knowledge of the true nature of God as well as the depth of the completeness of the salvation that Jesus Christ purchased for us on that cross at Calvary!

Let us consider this for a moment:

'I have said... *ye are gods*; and all of you are children of the most High but ye shall die like men, and fall like one of the princes.' (Psalm 82:6, 7; see also John 10:34, 35)

Does it surprise you that God calls you a "god"? What then, would make you "die like a man"?

The remedy to this lack of knowledge of God and His word is readily found in the scriptures, underscoring the need for a true worshipper to be fully acquainted with His word. Psalm 119 in its entirety is a good place to start in the journey of discovery of just how essential the knowledge of the word of God is. Jesus said: 'If ye abide in Me, and My words abide in you, ye shall ask what ye will and it shall be done unto you'. (John 15:7)

As a result of the lack of knowledge of the truth, a large number of Christians approach God more like a beggar than one who has been redeemed! Praise God, Jesus Christ made a new and living way for us, by which we are encouraged to "boldly approach the throne of grace".

Sadly, one of the major ways in which the TRUTH of God's word has been made ineffective in the life of Christians has been through the propagation and communication of erroneous doctrine, often via the medium of popular worship songs, repeated in Churches worldwide. Of course, the tendency for erroneous doctrine to spread within the body of Christ is exacerbated by too many Christians not taking the time to carefully study God's word for themselves. It is easy for information to be distorted when you do not take care to get it from the original source.

God knows the capability of the human mind and took this into consideration when He inspired the writers of the scriptures to pen those books. Many Hebrew scholars agree that much of the Hebrew Bible (Old Testament in the Christian Bible), is poetry. It is indeed evident that all the Psalms and Proverbs were written as poetry. Moreover, this poetry was not just spoken as we do today but was sung, acting as a perfect "aide memoire", making it relatively easy to memorise vast amounts of Scripture. Even today, young Jewish boys and girls preparing for their Bar Mitzvah and Bat Mitzvah respectively, have to learn by heart and "sing" certain parts of the Torah, (the first five books of the Bible) as part of the ceremony. Some children learn all five books verbatim by the time they have come of age at 12 years old for girls and 13 for boys. This is possible because these books, primarily written as poetry, are chanted in Hebrew which is the language in which they were originally written. Hebrew has neither vowels nor accents, meaning the Torah books have to be memorised using the correct melodies and pronunciations. The way to accomplish this is passed down from generation to generation. Therefore, it is not only necessary but also possible to get God's word written in our hearts. He already made a way for this to be achieved by every diligent student of His word.

The inherent power of music and songs to influence the minds of people is a tool that the enemy has been using for a very long time. Our heavenly Father, acknowledging how effectively songs can be used as a tool for disseminating information, instructed Moses, His servant: '...write this song and teach it to the people of Israel. Put it in their mouths, that this song may be a witness for me against the people of Israel' (Deuteronomy 31:19).

The failure to grasp the importance of our songs for worship or even songs tagged with the Christian label, has led to song lyrics which are rife with half-truths, and sentimental imagery set to beautiful melodies. These songs do not pass the scrutiny of the scriptures, yet they are taught and sung in churches everywhere, propagating an ever so slightly warped gospel each time, until no one identifies the God of the Bible as the one the song is purportedly speaking about! We must discern the subtle wiles of the devil; Satan himself is transformed into an angel of light. (2 Corinthians 11:14).

As Christians, we must engage our minds, an integral part of our souls in worship. We ought to take a moment to seriously consider what message that new, exciting, popular worship song is teaching. We should ask; does the message it promotes stand up to the scrutiny of God's word? Is what the song saying true? Does it glorify God or attempt to elevate man?

Some who have attempted to ask these questions have been accused of being unnecessarily pedantic in their approach. However, in much the same way that we are told to '...test the spirits to see whether they are from God' (1 John 4:1), I strongly believe that we should be like the Berean Christians and test what that latest hit worship song is saying with the yardstick of the word of God. While it is true that no one should give in to the temptation to become overly critical about everything, being specific and deliberate should be an important aspect of our daily Christian experience. I often remember the story of blind Bartimaeus, (Mark 10:46–52) the beggar who, on hearing that Jesus of Nazareth was passing by, cried out for mercy. Here is the kicker, when he got an audience with Jesus; Jesus asked him what he wanted. Why did Jesus ask that? Surely, it was obvious that the man desired the ability to see – yet, nothing happened until Bartimaeus articulated his specific desire to Jesus. It is not enough to be close enough. We must be specific. Our mortal enemy is strategic and deliberate about his plans and schemes to try to derail us.

We need to discern the times and seasons the Body of Christ lives in today. Perilous times in which, "...if it were possible" even the elect of God would be deceived.

The ONLY way to truly know God is through careful study of and meditation upon His word by the power of His Holy Spirit. It is time for us to be "wise as serpents".

The Father seeks...true worshippers:

Our God is not fooled by appearances; His Word is called a '...discerner of thoughts and the intents of the heart' (Hebrews 4:12).

The book of 1 Samuel, the 15th chapter, details how Saul, the king of Israel fell from grace when he disobeyed God's direct instruction to totally destroy all the Amalekites as well as all their possessions. Saul's obedience was partial, which equates to disobedience, as he did not destroy everything as he had been instructed, choosing to keep the best of the spoil for himself and the people (1 Samuel 15:9). Saul's disobedience caused God to remove both him and his generations after him from the throne; handing it over to David and his descendants forever.

As the prophet Samuel, said;

> *'Has the LORD as great delight in burnt offerings and sacrifices, as in obeying the voice of the LORD? Behold, to obey is better than sacrifice, and to listen than the fat of rams.' (1 Samuel 15: 22)*

God sees not as man sees, because He is looking into our hearts. He knows what we are thinking and even reveals our own hidden motives to us when we pay attention to His Word. Saul made the costly error of attempting to cover up his wrongdoing by making sacrifices which God had not prescribed, and when

that failed, he asked Samuel to help him to pretend everything was alright in the sight of the elders and the people of Israel:
'Then Saul pleaded again, I know I have sinned. But please, at least honour me before the elders of my people and before Israel by coming back with me so that I may worship the Lord your God.' (1 Samuel 15:30 NLT)
How often are we tempted even today to fall into that same error of judgement? Honouring God with our lips though our hearts are far from Him? God is not mocked; He has laid down the principle that a man will reap what he sows! Though many are keeping up appearances, God is not deceived in any way; instead, He has His own plan:

> *'For the eyes of the Lord are over the righteous, and His ears are open unto their prayers: but the face of the Lord is against them that do evil.' (1 Peter 3:12)*

This is a good place to emphasise the need for full honesty in our worship; in our relationship with God. He knows everything about us. Psalm 139 reminds us that there is nowhere to which we can run and hide; nowhere so far away that God cannot see us… He knows our thoughts from afar. However, we need not be deceived into believing that, if or when we mess up, we have to get right with God before we come to Him. Sadly, many have been deceived by an irrational logic that says, "I am too unclean to get into God's presence; I will wait until I sort myself out before I try to get back into His presence". This is an incorrect conclusion to arrive at because the only way to "get right" with God is to approach Him based on the sacrifice of our Lord Jesus. We cannot get right with God if we do not approach Him. We do have access to Him, but it's not because of our own imagined righteousness, but because of His righteousness. Depending on our own rightness or self-appointed goodness is an exercise in futility.

Furthermore, there is no need to echo the Psalmist (David) in Psalm 51:10, 'Create in me a clean heart, O God, and renew a right spirit within me.' We need to distinguish the marked differences between the Old and New Covenants. This is an integral aspect of worshipping in truth. Once we have been born-again, the Holy Spirit comes to dwell in us by faith. Our spirits are reborn; therefore, we should no longer approach God passively, expecting Him to come and create ***another*** new heart within us! What we are expected to do is to confess and forsake sin, receive His forgiveness, renew our minds with His word and thus be transformed.

We need to understand the grace of God which is solely dependent on the sacrifice Jesus Christ our Lord made on that cross at Calvary. We neither earn, nor deserve God's grace, it is a gift made available to us because of God's righteousness, and enables us to come ***boldly into God's presence...*** 'We may come near then, with freedom, to the throne of the grace, that we may receive kindness, and find grace– for seasonable help' (Hebrews 10:4 – YLT). The term "seasonable help" is rendered "help in time of need" in the KJV.

Praise God, we have access to help from God whenever we need it, not because we have been good people, but because of His loving-kindness.

POINTS TO PONDER

1. Do you agree that praise has to be vocalised or visual in order to count as praise or is there a different dimension you can think of?
2. From your personal experience; what do you think worship is?

3. Are you certain you are worshiping the one true God? What is your evidence for this?
4. Do you agree with the premise that man is made up of 3 distinct parts: spirit, soul and body? Do you think this distinction matters at all?
5. Do you agree that there is, or there should be a marked difference between Old Testament and New Testament worship?
6. Why is it important to worship God “in truth”? Can you give examples of true and false worship?

CHAPTER THREE

Enter His gates.

'Enter into His gates with thanksgiving, and into His courts with praise: be thankful unto Him and bless His Name.' (Psalm 100: 4)

Thanksgiving:

Seeing now that we have the confidence to boldly approach the throne of God by the blood of the Lamb, it is our responsibility to find out from His word the method of approach He prescribes. The verse above suggests that a proper way to enter God's presence is with a gratitude-filled heart. As the people of God who are approaching the great and mighty King, it is important to discover where our priorities should lie so that we can adjust our thinking, attitudes and actions accordingly.

A worshipper's life is full of praise and thanksgiving. The psalmist (David) says in Psalm 34:1 'I will ***bless the Lord at all times***; His praise shall continually be in my mouth'. This assertion illuminates an attitude of the heart which is worthy of emulation. Surely, if I determine to keep God's praise in my mouth continually, I will continually find reasons to praise Him!

Our priority is to present a life of unending praise and thanksgiving to God, a heart that truly appreciates that, without Him, we are nothing. Praise God that, as we have discovered, we are never without Him! Our self-centred hopes or dreams should pale into complete insignificance when we turn our eyes to God and see Him as He truly is; our Lord and King, the Creator of the heavens and the earth, and the One who continues to uphold all things by the Word of His power! Truly, it is of the Lord's mercies that we are not consumed (Lamentations 3:22). What if God were to withhold His breath from our nostrils? This is a sobering thought which should help to bring our thinking to the correct perspective each time we are tempted to complain instead of praise and give thanks.

We must remember that God is always deserving of our high praise (unrestrained, exuberant and loud praise!). Indeed, the more we deliberately find the innumerable reasons we have for thanking Him, the more we see the enemy defeated. Satan is defeated because his strategy fails – we are no longer without hope as we look back on what God has already done. We then gain confidence that He can, and will do it again. A well rehearsed (and executed) ploy of the enemy, used to great effect for millennia; is to use whatever he can to distract us. Therefore, for as long as we focus on things we want but do not have, we are deceived into forgetting to identify and be deliberately thankful for what we do posses.

The importance of a life of gratitude cannot be overemphasised. Scripture is full of words of admonition and encouragement, teaching us to develop a grateful heart.

One of the signs of the "last days" revealed in the scriptures is that men would, amongst other things, be unthankful:

> *'For men shall be lovers of their own selves, covetous, boasters, proud, blasphemers, disobedient to parents,* ***unthankful****, unholy, without natural affection, trucebreakers, false accusers, incontinent, fierce, despisers of those that are good, traitors, heady, high minded, lovers of pleasures more than lovers of God; having a form of godliness but denying the power thereof: from such turn away.'(2 Timothy 3:2 – 5)*

Any true follower of Christ who is aware of world news reports will concede that much of global occurrences today, directly fulfill the scripture above. More importantly, we need to heed the word of God, ensuring that we do not fall into the trap of taking His grace on our lives for granted.

Luke 17:11–19 tells the story of the ten lepers who encountered God's grace in the person of Jesus Christ:

> *'And it came to pass, as He went to Jerusalem that He passed through the midst of Samaria and Galilee. And as He entered into a certain village, there met Him ten men that were lepers, which stood afar off: and they lifted up their voices, and said, "Jesus, Master, have mercy on us." And when He saw them, He said unto them, "Go shew yourselves unto the priests." And it came to pass, that, as they went, they were cleansed. And one of them, when he saw that he was healed, turned back, and with a loud voice glorified God, and fell down on his face at his feet, giving Him thanks: and he was a Samaritan. And Jesus answering said, "were there not ten cleansed? but where are the nine? There are not found that returned to give glory to God, save this stranger." And He said unto him, "Arise, go thy way: thy faith hath made thee whole."'*

How often do we yield to the temptation to behave like the nine lepers in the passage above? All ten lepers were healed, cleansed of their leprosy... as they went. As they obeyed the Word spoken to them, they received what they had asked of the Lord. We can also surmise that the other nine lepers were Israelites, as the tenth man was specifically identified as a Samaritan. The Samaritan saw he was healed, turned back and 'with a loud voice, glorified God'. He was grateful, his gratitude immediately evident. He saw that he was healed, then:

1. He turned back
2. With a loud voice, glorified God
3. Fell on his face at Jesus' feet
4. He gave thanks

Why was this man so grateful? Why was he the only one who came back to give thanks? Could it be that he was the only one who discerned that his healing was undeserved? Did he identify this as the unmerited favour of God on them? Were the other nine not as grateful because they felt THEY deserved this grace – they were of the seed of Abraham after all?

The Samaritan's gratitude earned him extra. All ten were cleansed, but he was the only one to whom Jesus said, 'Thy faith hath made thee whole'. Wholeness, completeness, came as a result of his faith. Note that Jesus identified the Samaritan's gratitude as "faith".

In another account in Luke 7, Jesus spoke to Simon the Pharisee who was shocked at Jesus' response when 'a woman in the city, which was a sinner' anointed His feet with an alabaster box of ointment. He told the parable of a creditor and two debtors; one who was forgiven little, and the other who was forgiven much, asking which one would love more. Jesus concluded by saying:

'Wherefore I say unto thee, her sins, which are many, are forgiven; for she loved much: but to who little is forgiven, *the same* loveth little.' (Luke 7:47).

Do we truly believe we have only little to be forgiven of? If not, why then are we not as thankful as we could, or should be? I have heard several people on different occasions say things like: "well, I asked God for this thing and I didn't get it, so I told God I was angry with Him". Sadly, those who speak this way do not see anything wrong with their reaction. In fact, their ability to convey their private annoyance to God in this manner seems to give them a strange sense of extra intimacy with God. To me as an observer, people who say they have told God that they are angry with Him appear to be rather smug about it. In my opinion, those who react this way are displaying shallow immaturity rather than a deep walk with God. Do we ever think about the children of Israel in the wilderness, who, having seen the great and mighty things God had done on their behalf would immediately start to murmur and complain as soon as they encountered some difficulty? A lot of people believe that if they had lived in the times when Jesus walked the earth as the Son of Man, they would have recognised Him as King and not denied Him. I wonder how true this claim is, seeing that we are living in the dispensation of a much better Covenant than those who lived in those times did! In the new Covenant, we have the Holy Spirit living inside us! In contrast, the Holy Spirit "came upon" just the prophets of old, and that was in order to perform a specific task. With the Holy Spirit inside us as born again believers, we have access to the same power that raised our Lord Jesus Christ from the dead – on a constant basis! He is sent to us to be our teacher and guide, leading us into all truth and reminding us of God's specific promises to us at the appropriate time. We may however fail to realise how we effectively stop God's power from working within and through us when we constantly complain and murmur. Consequently, though the same power that raised Jesus from the dead lives in us, doubt and unbelief, evidenced in murmuring and complaining; prevents our true potential from being realised.

Surely, there is a reason the scriptures repeatedly encourage us to be thankful. God is not an egomaniac. Could His reason for asking us to be thankful be that cultivating a grateful heart predisposes us to receive more?

'In everything give thanks: for this is the will of God in Christ Jesus concerning you.' (1 Thessalonians 5:18)

This is a noteworthy assertion: the solution to whatever challenge we face in life can be found in God's word, as long as we allow His Spirit to illuminate our hearts. The Psalmist says in Psalm 43:5, 'Why art thou cast down, O my soul? And why art thou disquieted within me? Hope in God: for I shall yet praise Him, who is the health of my countenance, and my God.' Is there a better cure for a downcast heart than to take one's mind off one's self, and deliberately choose to focus on God's goodness in our lives instead? We must challenge the lies of the enemy which say nothing is going right, or says that no one loves us. If we look at these lies objectively, we will see them for what they are, mere distractions deliberately sent to divert our attention away from the truth of God's promises. The devil wants to steal our joy and peace, but he cannot have his way if we would only hold on to God's promises, knowing He is a faithful God who wants to prosper us, rather than bring us to harm.

A life of worship is a lifestyle of thanksgiving, always recognising God's hand in every area of our lives. In fact, a true worshipper is ALWAYS thankful, seeking to give honour to God for even the most seemingly mundane things in his or her life. We must avoid engaging in "idolatry", seeking God only for what we may receive from Him, rather than because He is worthy.

Enter His courts with Praise:

If you can, right where you are as you read this, look up to the sky, breathe in deeply and take a moment to consciously observe the wonders of creation. Do you feel a stirring in your heart? Do you feel an urge to burst out in praise? Does a feeling of awe seem to encompass you? Or do you feel ...nothing? An unfortunate downside to living in a major city in these modern times is that most of us seem to forget to take a little time, every so often, and just look up to the heavens.

'...The heavens declare the glory of God; and the firmament sheweth His handiwork.' (Psalm 19:1)

'For since the creation of the world, God's invisible qualities, His eternal power and divine nature, have been clearly seen, being understood from His workmanship, so that men are without excuse.' (Romans 1:20)

The greatness of God's power is evident in the things He created. Therefore, the only reason many do not give Him the glory that is due is that they have been blinded. People are unable to see through the lie and sheer implausibility of the Universe without the Master Designer, for example, because 'the god of this world hath blinded the minds of them which believe not, lest the light of the glorious gospel of Christ, who is the image of God, should shine unto them.'(2 Corinthians 4:4)

God is worthy of our praise and that is reason enough to praise Him. However, true to His nature of love, He has attached so many more benefits to our praise. It is no wonder then, that the scriptures are full of the command to 'Praise the Lord'.

We are called to 'show forth His praise'

1 Peter 2:9 tells us that we (those who follow Christ Jesus) are '...a chosen generation, a royal priesthood, a holy nation, a peculiar people; that ye should shew forth the praises of Him who hath called you out of darkness into His marvellous light'. God ransomed us from the kingdom of darkness and translated us into the Kingdom of His dear Son. He did this so that we might declare His praises before the Gentiles, the unbelievers, the heathen. Jesus calls those He has redeemed by His own blood, "the light of the world", "the salt of the earth", "a city that is set on a hill that cannot be hidden"; encouraging us to let our light shine before men, that they might see our good works and ***glorify God in Heaven***!

When He was leaving the earth, Jesus asked His disciples to 'wait for the promise of the Father' (Acts 1:4b), and by the next chapter, we read about the day of Pentecost, when the disciples were filled with the Holy Ghost and began to speak with other tongues as the Holy Spirit enabled them. In the eleventh verse of Acts 2, we discover that the multitudes present were confounded at what was going on, because they heard the disciples '...speak in our tongues the ***wonderful works of God***'. The disciples were declaring God's praises in other tongues, in the midst of the multitude of people who were still unbelievers at the time!

God inhabits the praises of His people:

'But thou art holy, O thou that inhabitest the praises of Israel.' (Psalm 22:3)

It is evident through the scriptures that God enjoys our praise, He chooses to inhabit (some other translations say He is enthroned on) the praises of Israel.

In Genesis, we read about Leah, Jacob's wife. Jacob did not love Leah; instead, he loved her sister, Rachel. Leah, after naming her other children from her place of hurt, finally turned her focus to God and chose to call her last-born son Judah. Leah said: '...Now will I praise the LORD: therefore, she called his name **Judah**; and left bearing.' (Genesis 29:35b)

The name Judah which is "Yehudah", in Hebrew, means "Praise". When we trace the lineage of Judah, we realise that God placed special favour upon that tribe. In Psalm 78, for example, we are told that God rejected the tent of Joseph; He did not choose the tribe of Ephraim;

> *'But chose the tribe of Judah, the mount Zion which He loved. And He built His sanctuary like high palaces, like the earth which He hath established forever.' (Psalm 78:68 – 69)*

Verse 69 above once again reiterates that God chooses to build His tabernacle, His dwelling place, His sanctuary, upon the praises of His people. He decides to remain in the company of those who praise Him.

God chose the tribe of Judah, the tribe from which our Lord, the Messiah came. Indeed, Jesus Christ, the Anointed One is called 'The Lion of the Tribe of Judah'. Moreover, king David, whom

God called 'a man after my own heart' was a descendant of this especially favoured tribe.

If we were to do a little exercise, substituting the word "praise" for Judah in some passages of scripture, an interesting pattern emerges:

In Psalm 76, for example, we read; "In Judah is God known: His name is great in Israel. In Salem also is His tabernacle, and His dwelling place in Zion."

The substitution of the name "Judah" for the word praise was introduced and thoroughly explained in the book "Exploring Worship; a practical guide to praise and Worship by Bob Sorge. (Sorge, Published April 1st 1987)

Using our substitution method above, the passage now becomes: In the company of those who praise, God is known; His name is great in Israel (Israel meaning the general assembly).

Note the distinction made between the tribe of Judah and the entirety of Israel in that verse. God shows a distinction between the children of Israel and His chosen one, Moses as recorded in Psalm 103:

'He made known His ways unto Moses, His acts unto the children of Israel.' (Psalm 103:7).

We ought to understand something of God's nature in this regard; that while He is not partial, and everyone who comes to God through our Lord Jesus Christ is accepted of Him, He will show His favour to those who fully follow Him. Everyone who is called by His Name has equal access to Him.

There are several examples in scripture of the distinctions God makes; the special favour He shows to specific people in both the Old and New Testaments. For instance, we read:

'Enoch walked with God: and he was not; for God took him' (Genesis 5:24);

'And the LORD said, Shall I hide from Abraham that thing which I do?' (Genesis 18:17)

'The secret of the LORD *is* with them that fear Him; and He will shew them His covenant.' (Psalm 25:14)
'Henceforth I call you not servants; for the servant knoweth not what his lord doeth: but I have called you friends; for all things that I have heard of My Father I have made known unto you.' (John 15:15)
The preceding passages show us that *we* determine how far we go in our relationship with God. This is a choice we make daily, consciously or otherwise. God says we should draw near to Him and He would draw near to us (James 4:8). Therefore, when we live a life of thanksgiving and praise, accompanied by the understanding that this is God's will for us, we can begin to occupy our God-intended positions as kings and priests of the Most High. We belong to the class of people who God permits to offer sacrifices to Him. Hallelujah!
As we carefully study the scriptures, we discover that there are many dimensions to our praise; and several things our God accomplishes through us as we praise Him.

God's tangible presence:

True praise often invokes the tangible presence of God. God is omnipresent; He is present everywhere, but notably, in the New Covenant, He 'tabernacles' or lives within us by His Spirit. Distinctively though, the tangible presence of God is something we can sense in this physical realm and this is true both in the Old and within the New Covenants.
In the New Covenant, God's presence dwells in individuals by faith, once we have been born-again. In the Old Covenant, however, His presence was not within His people all the time. His Spirit "came upon" individuals when He wanted them to perform specific tasks. His presence was also revealed to the entire congregation to effect a measurable outcome. Thus, God chose to reveal His presence as a pillar of cloud by day and a

pillar of fire by night as He led the children of Israel out of Egypt into the Promised Land (Exodus 13:21–22). In both the Old and New covenants, He chooses to reveal His presence in a tangible way which we can discern with our physical senses.

The account in 2 Chronicles 5:12–14 describes God's manifest presence as the priests began to praise God in unity:

> *'and the Levites who were the singers, all those of Asaph and Heman and Jeduthun, with their sons and their brethren, stood at the east end of the altar, clothed in white linen, having cymbals, stringed instruments and harps, and with them one hundred and twenty priests sounding with trumpets— indeed it came to pass, when the trumpeters and singers were as one, to make one sound to be heard in praising and thanking the Lord, and when they lifted up their voice with the trumpets and cymbals and instruments of music, and praised the Lord, saying: "For He is good, For His mercy endures forever," that the house, the house of the Lord, was filled with a cloud, so that the priests could not continue ministering because of the cloud; for the glory of the Lord filled the house of God'. (NKJV)*

Having offered sacrifices, the Levites praised God, declaring His goodness and faithfulness. God's presence filled the house, so much so that the priests could no longer stand to perform their duties.

A particularly explosive manifestation of God inhabiting the praises of His people is recorded in the book of Acts chapter 16:25, 26)

> *'And at midnight Paul and Silas prayed, and sang praises unto God: and the prisoners heard them. And suddenly there was a great earthquake so that the foundations of the prison were shaken: and immediately all the doors were opened, and everyone's bands were loosed.'*

There is no doubt that this was indeed a fantastic demonstration of the Lord's tangible presence as He chose to inhabit the praises of His servants. Chains were broken, fetters loosed, those bound were set free. These are all wonderful effects of praising our God in the beauty of His Holiness.

A word of caution is appropriate here. Each time we approach the Father of lights, we must examine our motives and adjust our hearts accordingly. Many have fallen into the error of seeking for signs and wonders rather than seeking God Almighty, the Creator of *All* things! The difference is subtle, but an error here can give birth to catastrophic consequences. This is where deception lives! The scriptures warn us that the enemy has a lot of lying signs and wonders at his disposal. When we consider the season we are in, in view of the timeline of God's eternal plan, we should surely conclude that we are in the "last days". We should, therefore, heed the warning written in 2 Thessalonians 2:9:

'The coming of the lawless one is by the activity of Satan with all power and false signs and wonders…'

Those who solely seek after signs and wonders are embarking on a risky undertaking.

First, it demonstrates a lack of faith in God who said, 'Blessed are those who have not seen, yet have believed' (John 20:29). Seeking after signs opens the seeker up to contrary spirits and demonic influences from Satan's cohorts. This is why we are told in 1 John 4:1 to test every spirit to see if they have come from God. If we consider Moses in Egypt and remember that Pharaoh's magicians were able to replicate most of the signs Moses displayed before him, we might appreciate the gravity of this warning. The litmus test for every sign, wonder or other supernatural experience is God's word, and this is why knowledge of the word is the incontrovertible key for every believer in Christ.

While examining what we refer to as the tangible presence of God, we should realise that: The Holy Spirit lives inside us (those who, by faith in Christ Jesus, have received the indwelling of the Holy Spirit) and is therefore present with us all the time. Our ability to sense His presence is more a function of our "tuning in" to (or becoming more aware of) His presence, rather than God suddenly becoming more present.

A great deal has been said in recent times about the "presence of God" being manifest in believers' assemblies in physical forms. Our considered approach should be to test everything in the light of God's word. I am persuaded that God's tangible presence would normally bring about quantifiable results and accomplish an identifiable purpose just as we see in the scriptures. Additionally, we should always check our motivation, ensuring that we are seeking the One who sends the signs and not just seeking the signs alone.

POINTS TO PONDER

1. With the benefit of hindsight, can you see specific instances when the devil succeeded in distracting you from achieving a particular goal? Or perhaps you were just delayed unnecessarily?
2. Can you think of any instances in the past where you have "experienced" God's tangible presence but are now not so sure if that was truly what it was? Or perhaps you heard stories of God's presence being in some meetings which prompted you to travel to seek such experiences? What is the "litmus test" for discerning God's presence or that He is indeed the One speaking to you?
3. Do you think you can rely on your feelings in order to discern God's presence accurately?

CHAPTER FOUR

Praise is a weapon

Once you have been born-again by the power of the Holy Spirit, you are automatically engaged in God's army. Our Lord Jesus revealed Himself to Joshua as "The commander" of His Army:

> *'...And He said, "No; but I am the commander of the army of the LORD. Now I have come." And Joshua fell on his face to the earth and worshipped and said to him, "What does my lord say to his servant?" And the commander of the LORD's army said to Joshua, "Take off your sandals from your feet, for the place where you are standing is holy." And Joshua did so.' (Joshua 5:14–15 ESV)*

We deduce that this was an incarnation of Jesus Christ, rather than an angel, because Joshua was not forbidden to worship this "person", even though the scriptures expressly forbid the worship of angels (see Exodus 20:4–5, Matthew 4:10, Luke 4:8).

Moreover, Joshua was given the same command God gave to Moses at the burning bush at Horeb: 'Then He said, "Do not come near; *take your sandals off your feet, for the place on which you are standing is holy ground.*"'(Exodus 3:5 ESV).

Since there is a commander, there is also an army. We must realise, therefore, that we have been drafted into this army and are engaged in warfare. This is not warfare in the natural sense, it is not in the flesh – not in the physical world. It is a spiritual war, fought in the realms that we cannot physically see. Paul's letter to the Ephesians states:

> *'Finally, my brethren, be strong in the Lord, and in the power of his might. Put on the whole armour of God that ye may be able to stand against the wiles of the devil. For we wrestle not against flesh and blood, but against principalities, against powers, against the rulers of the darkness of this world, against spiritual wickedness in high places. Wherefore take unto you the whole armour of God that ye may be able to withstand in the evil day, and having done all, to stand.' (Ephesians 6:10 –13)*

Now, because we are engaged in a spiritual battle, God has given us the appropriate armour with which to defend ourselves against assaults of the enemy. He also gave us the weapon with which we can launch our own offensive strikes – '***the sword of the Spirit*** – which is the word of God' (Ephesians 6:17b).

The position of praise as a weapon of warfare is repeatedly demonstrated in the lives of God's people, particularly in the Old Testament. We will be looking at a few of these instances in some detail.

Praise confuses the enemy – King Jehoshaphat

In the book of 2 Chronicles 20, we read of how the Moabites and the Ammonites gathered against the children of Judah. Jehoshaphat king of Judah assembled the people and prayed, reminding God about the covenant He made with Abraham. In direct response to this prayer, the Spirit of God came upon one of the Levites, giving specific directions about how to engage the enemy:

> *'Then upon Jahaziel the son of Zechariah, the son of Benaiah, the son of Jeiel, the son of Mattaniah, a Levite of the sons of*

> *Asaph, came the Spirit of the LORD in the midst of the congregation; And he said, Hearken ye, all Judah, and ye inhabitants of Jerusalem, and thou king Jehoshaphat, Thus saith the LORD unto you, Be not afraid nor dismayed by reason of this great multitude; for the battle is not yours, but God's. Tomorrow go ye down against them: behold, they come up by the cliff of Ziz; and ye shall find them at the end of the brook, before the wilderness of Jeruel.* ***Ye shall not need to fight in this battle: set yourselves, stand ye still, and see the salvation of the LORD*** *with you, O Judah and Jerusalem: fear not, nor be dismayed; tomorrow go out against them: for the LORD will be with you. And Jehoshaphat bowed his head with his face to the ground: and all Judah and the inhabitants of Jerusalem fell before the LORD, worshipping the LORD. And the Levites, of the children of the Kohathites, and of the children of the Korhites, stood up to praise the LORD God of Israel with a loud voice on high.' (2 Chronicles 20:14 – 19).*

Notice that as soon as they heard these words of comfort and direction, all the congregation, (including the king) fell before the Lord, worshipping Him, then the Levites (the priests) stood up to praise the Lord God.

They praised God based on His promise through Jahaziel that they would experience His salvation, even though this particular promise was yet to materialise. Praising God for the answer *before* you have seen the manifestation of His promise, helps to establish that promise in your heart. Praising God in this situation is an act of **faith;** faith being the 'evidence of things not seen'. When you praise God for answers yet unseen, you are 'calling the things that be not as though they were' (Romans 4:17).

Our Lord Jesus showed us the converse of this principle of His Kingdom when He said in Matthew 6:31 – '*Therefore take no thought, saying, what shall we eat? or, what shall we drink? or, Wherewithal shall we be clothed?'* He was indicating to us that negative thoughts become a reality when we say them out loud. Other translations render that phrase as: 'don't be anxious saying...' The principle is the same: just as we have been told that we give life to God's promises by confessing (saying) them, it works equally in the negative. We give life to anxieties and contrary thoughts if we say or meditate on them long enough. The responsibility is therefore on us to align the words we speak, sing and meditate upon with God's truth alone.

In the new covenant, we discover that we have a 'more sure word of prophecy' (2 Peter 1:19–20) that is; we have the Holy Scriptures. Furthermore, we also have the indwelling of the Holy Spirit and can depend on God to keep His promises. He is God, and will not change, and His Spirit bears witness with our spirits that we are sons of God. Hallelujah!

As we continue to the conclusion of this account which relates how God used the weapon of praise to completely confuse the enemies of His people; we see Jehoshaphat the king rallying the children of Judah. The incomprehensible occurred! The king of Judah appointed singers to praise God, and sent them out ahead of the army!

> *'...And when he had consulted with the people, he appointed singers unto the LORD, and that should praise the beauty of holiness, as they went out before the army, and to say, Praise the LORD; for his mercy endureth forever.* ***And when they began to sing and to praise, the LORD set ambushments against the children of Ammon, Moab, and mount Seir, which were come against Judah; and they were smitten.*** *For the children of Ammon and Moab stood up against the inhabitants of mount Seir, utterly to slay and destroy them: and when they had made an end of the inhabitants of Seir, everyone helped to destroy another.' (2 Chronicles 20:21–23)*

As the children of Judah praised Jehovah, the LORD ambushed their enemies! Oh, that we would accept that God will fight our battles if we would praise Him for His goodness, His promises, and for who He is. If we would take our focus off the giants that confront us and fix our gaze on the One who has promised us abundant life, He has said the battle belongs to Him; He will fight for us and we will hold our peace (Exodus 14:14).

Praise confuses the enemy - Gideon's army

In Judges Chapter 7, we read the story of Gideon (called the mighty man of valour) and how the Lord God used him –along with 300 men only, to defeat the Midianite armies (including the Amalekites and the children of the east who '*...lay along in the valley like grasshoppers for multitude; and their camels were without number, as the sand by the seaside for multitude.'* Judges 7:12)

There are several lessons to learn from this event. First, God deliberately used a small army to defeat the enemy. In doing this, He showed that, when we are on the Lord's side, we are on the winning side. This is regardless of the multitude of enemies we may be facing or how seemingly insurmountable our problems are. He said to Gideon, 'The people with you are too many for Me to give the Midianites into their hand, lest Israel boast over me, saying, "My own hand has saved me."' (Judges 7:2 ESV)

After taking Gideon's army through a series of tests, God whittled the army down from 22,000 to just 300 men, ensuring that all the glory would be His alone. This presents a good reminder for us to examine our individual lives and ask; "Am I attempting to take a share of the glory that belongs to God alone? What is my motivation in all I do? Am I trying to expand His kingdom or am I building my own?"

God worked out a great victory for the children of Israel against the vast Midianite army through Gideon's obedience. All Gideon and his army had to do was to obey God, and with their arsenal comprising trumpets, torches and victorious shouts, their enemies were completely disoriented such that we read:

'When they blew the 300 trumpets, the Lord set every man's sword against his comrade and against all the army' (Judges 7:22 ESV). The Midianite army fought against each other – remember, there were no swords in the hands of Gideon's army!

Walls tumble down

Another instance where the children of Israel, the Lord's chosen people, utilized the weapon of praise is recorded in the 6th chapter of the book of Joshua. Joshua, in obedience to God's instruction, was to lead the children of Israel into the inheritance previously promised to them. Note that the Promised Land was already occupied, yet God told Joshua, 'I have given into thine hand Jericho, and the king thereof, and the mighty men of valour.' (Joshua 6:2)

Once again, a dramatic victory accomplished for the children of God is preceded by a promise, a specific instruction from God, and a victorious shout of praise! This time, the Lord commanded that the Israelite armed troops march just ahead of seven priests blowing seven trumpets in front of the Ark of the Covenant. Once a day for six days, the children of Israel, led by the armed troops and priests, silently marched around the wall of the city of Jericho. On the seventh day, however, they marched in silence six times, then gave a great shout of victory as the priests blew on their trumpets the seventh time!

> *'So the people shouted when the priests blew with the trumpets: and it came to pass, when the people heard the sound of the trumpet, and the people shouted with a great shout, that the wall fell down flat, so that the people went up into the city, every man straight before him, and they took the city.' (Joshua 6:20).*

The walls fell down as the Israelites raised their voices in a shout of victory. This was a victory they had been promised, and they saw its manifestation as they completed their obedience.

The shout of victory is often mentioned in the Psalms. The victorious shout says in essence; "Lord, we are not looking at our situations or the adverse circumstances that confront us. Rather, our eyes are on You, on Your goodness, Your grace and Your mercy. We rely on Your promise; and we know that You are faithful, therefore, we have the answer to our petitions. We have the victory, so we shout Your praises in advance of seeing the answer physically come to pass."

Of course, this attitude may appear to onlookers as counting our proverbial chickens before they are hatched; however, it is a demonstration of faith. We can shout victoriously because we are "calling the things that be not as though they were". We rejoice before we have seen the answer just as much as we would if we were seeing the answer physically! This attitude confuses the enemy, as we saw in the story of king Jehoshaphat in 2 Chronicles 23 where it is said of the children of Moab and Ammon: "everyone helped to destroy another"; they turned against each other, so that they were annihilated. The children of Judah did not have to fight in that battle.

God seems to have chosen this weapon of praise as chief of His instruments, His preferred tool, for engineering the discomfiture, disorientation and eventual destruction of His enemies and the enemies of His people. God also designed His protection for His people such that those who rise up against us end up defeating themselves. Hallelujah! (See Proverbs 26:27; Psalm 141:10, Psalm 7:15)

Perhaps one of the most explicit passages of scripture describing praise as a weapon for warfare is found in Psalm 149:

> *'Let the high praises of God be in their mouth, and a two-edged sword in their hand; To execute vengeance upon the heathen, and punishments upon the people; To bind their kings with chains, and their nobles with fetters of iron; To execute upon them the judgment written; this honour have all His saints. Praise ye the LORD.'*

This is worthy of due consideration; that God Himself tells us to praise Him. He calls us to offer high praise to Him and, having the two-edged sword in our hands, go to war against His enemies. We know that the two-edged sword mentioned here alludes to God's Word which is even 'sharper than any two-edged sword' (Hebrews 4:12). When we think of the term "high praise", the image that comes to mind should include loud noise, dancing, and exuberant joy being offered to God. High praise involves behaving in an unmeasured way. Think of your favourite team winning a keenly contested game at the final whistle. At that point, you do not even think about, let alone care, that anyone is looking at you. The sole focus of your attention at that moment is that your favourite team won. Most people would shout, dance and become animated. Why then do many stand still during a congregational worship service? We are assured of victory in Christ Jesus; why then do we withhold our praise? Some allow their minds to wander and do not connect with what is going on, others may be preoccupied with thoughts of challenges they are facing and find it difficult to focus their troubled minds on praising God. The onus is then placed on the worship leaders to get them to give God the praise that He is due.

All too often in congregational worship, an undue amount of pressure is placed upon the worship team. Some people appear to rationalise the way they engage with congregational worship with thinking that says: "if the worship team does well today, if they play those favourite worship songs of mine, or if my preferred worship leader is leading the worship, I will join in; if not, then I will just stand or sit. It all depends on how I feel."

The truth is that if we all, as priests unto God, learn to privately develop a lifestyle of worship and praise, the job of the worship leader would be made much simpler when we come together. We would come together as one Body, in tune with the voice of

God's Holy Spirit during our worship services and no longer require anyone to cajole us to worship.

There is little doubt that having a Spirit-filled and experienced worship leader and music team can (and does) help lead a congregation into a glorious time of worship and praise. We must, however, remain conscious that we have come to worship Almighty God rather than satisfy ourselves. There is no need to wait for optimal conditions for worship before lifting our hearts and voices in praise and worship. Our worship is to and for Him. May God open our spiritual eyes so we may truly see, just as the prophet Elisha prayed that God would open his servant Gehazi's "eyes" to see God's provision for their protection:

> *'Then Elisha prayed and said, "O LORD, please open his eyes that he may see." So the LORD opened the eyes of the young man, and he saw, and behold, the mountain was full of horses and chariots of fire all around Elisha.' 2 Kings 6:17)*

What we connect with via our physical senses is but a limited component of the expanse of all that God created! While we are looking at the worship band or choir from a natural perspective, for instance, we may not fully perceive that so much more is going on. The Bible gives us some insight in the book of Hebrews 12:18:

'For ye are not come unto the mount that might be touched, and that burned with fire, nor unto blackness, and darkness, and tempest...'

Although we assemble in a physical location, we are actually relocating spiritually. We are approaching the presence of God Himself, before His throne in Heaven. This is the City of God where the heavenly hosts, the saints that have gone ahead of us, all reside! What an awesome privilege. Hallelujah!

> *'But ye are come unto mount Sion, and unto the city of the living God, the heavenly Jerusalem, and to an innumerable company of angels to the general assembly and church of the*

> *firstborn, which are written in heaven, and to God the Judge of all, and to the spirits of just men made perfect, and to Jesus the mediator of the new covenant, and to the blood of sprinkling, that speaketh better things than that of Abel.' (Hebrews 12:22–24).*

Understanding this truth makes a plausible argument for closed eyes as an appropriate posture for worship. At the very least, our ability to focus is enhanced.

Remember, as children of God, we have been drafted into the Lord's army. It is no longer a question of choice. As a result, God, not willing to leave us defenceless, has provided weapons for us to wield. These are not physical weapons, because the enemy we are engaging with is not in this physical realm, but praise God, the weapons given to us for our warfare are: 'mighty through God to the pulling down of strongholds; casting down imaginations, and every high thing that exalteth itself against the knowledge of God, and bringing into captivity every thought to the obedience of Christ;' (2 Corinthians 10:4–5).

Our praise, our adoration of God is one such weapon. In fact, praising God is a particularly potent mode of spiritual warfare as we have seen in several scriptural references. Moreover, our ability to praise God is an honour and privilege that God has bestowed on His people. As heirs of the Father and joint heirs with the Son, we execute the judgement God has written. Choosing to praise God in the face of contrary circumstances establishes our focus on His promises, rather than on adverse situations or challenges. Praise is a demonstration of our faith in God, showing our trust in His faithfulness, assured that, what He has promised, He is faithful to perform.

POINTS TO PONDER

---

1. How did you come to the realisation that Christians are enlisted into the Army of The Lord? Are you sure you are part of that army?
2. Do you agree with the premise that praise is a weapon?
3. Apart from the "weapon" of praise discussed here; what other weapons has God given to the believer? Can you differentiate between the offensive weapons and defensive ones?
4. Can you think of a time in your life when you deliberately chose the weapon of praise? Did you see a measurable outcome?

Chapter 5:

Songs of the Lord; – singing and writing songs of worship.

Sing unto Him a new song; play skilfully with a loud noise. (Psalm 33:3)

One day, sooner than many of us realise, those who have put their faith in Jesus Christ alone will be transformed. We will be changed from mortal to immortality so that we can fully know our God and be with Him forever.

One of the main occupations we will have then, according to the Scriptures, is worshipping Him. We will all be involved in praising Him, joining with brothers and sisters from every nation, tribe and tongue. We will, with the hosts of heaven, form the great multitude shouting and singing His praises forever. Here on Earth, it seems we have a practice run, a shadow of things to come. What we have now is a small taste or a preview of what is to come, indeed, what is already happening in Heaven right now! The book of Psalms encourages God's people to praise Him all the time: "I will bless the Lord at all times, His praise shall continually be in my mouth" (Psalm34:1). This call to praise is carried on into the New Testament, where we are further encouraged to sing psalms and hymns and spiritual songs, making melody in our hearts unto God (Ephesians 5:19, Colossians 3:16).

In the book of Revelation, we read about the 24 elders who, along with the four living creatures, fell down before the Lamb of God **"...and they sang a new song"** (Revelation 5:9). As we study the scriptures, we discover that there is, even now, a choir of heavenly hosts who are constantly singing, speaking and declaring God's praises in heaven. Here on Earth, God's children are also supposed to praise Him continually, while our lives bring praise and honour unto Him. God declared in Isaiah 43:21 "This people have I formed for Myself; they shall show forth My praise".

David followed a pattern of what is going on in heaven right now when he appointed temple musicians who were engaged in the "work" of praising God all day and all night. These were skilled musicians and singers, enlisted in this ministry in order to constantly declare the praises of God.

The Bible assures us that God inhabits the praises of His people (Psalm 22:3). He decides to tabernacle, to live – with us, the ones He created. Think about this for a moment; God, the Creator of the Heavens and the earth, chooses to make the praises you and I offer to Him, a "place" where He dwells!

Several times in scripture, we are shown examples of what the physical manifestation of God dwelling in the praises of His people could look like. This is not to encourage us to seek after signs, but to demonstrate the love our heavenly Father will lavish on those who choose to praise Him, giving Him the honour He is due.

What are you listening to?

Much like the other things God has given us to enjoy, the ability to not only create but appreciate beautiful music is another precious gift from Him. A significant portion of the Bible was inspired as poetry to be sung; demonstrating the special place God has in His heart for the songs we sing to Him.

Within the confines of this chapter, we will concern ourselves with the content of the songs we sing and listen to, which then take prominent places in our subconscious whether we acknowledge this fact or not. The scriptures encourage God's people to sing a new song unto the Lord, to sing psalms, hymns and spiritual songs to one another and to make melodies in our hearts unto God. What we might fail to realise, however, is how much the songs we sing or consistently listen to, can shape or even determine our moods, our theology and what goes on within our daily lives. Whether or not many mainstream Christian songwriters appreciate this fact remains unclear, if one were to judge by the songs which are heralded as songs of faith, but fail woefully when examined in the light of the Holy Scriptures.

This is a good place to pause and think about our lives. We have just read that what we listen to, meditate upon, and give voice to, all have the potential to create or form our experiences. We are warned in Proverbs 4:23, "watch over your heart with all diligence, for from it flows the springs of life" (NASB). This is further expounded in Philippians 4:8:

> *"Finally, brethren, whatsoever things are true, whatsoever things are honest, whatsoever things are just, whatsoever things are pure, whatsoever things are lovely, whatsoever things are of good report; if there be any virtue, if there be any praise, think on these things."*

Crucially, many Christians do not appear to understand the potent power wielded by the songs we listen to. The repetitive nature of most songs helps to keep the words firmly entrenched within our minds, whether we pay attention to the process or not. Many of us subject ourselves to an onslaught of doubt, depression, rage, perversion and a plethora of evil; just because we are not selective in the songs we consistently listen to. For too many, our focus is more on how trendy and high up in the charts our favourite songs are, or the musical innovation that was introduced. It appears a lot of us consider anything but the extent of psychological damage to which we may be willfully exposing ourselves. As Christians, we should at least aspire to use Philippians 4:8 as our yardstick, particularly for any secular songs we listen to.

An understanding of the differences between the types of songs we sing is desirable, where we look to emphasise content alongside tempo and musical genre. Placing due emphasis should help inform songwriters, worship leaders and the general congregation on whether particular songs are appropriate or not. In a worship service for example, we could have songs for praise, worship and adoration, songs of rejoicing, dedication, supplication, and songs for repentance. There is a place for each of these types of songs and that should be evident to a worship leader who is led by the Holy Spirit and is aware of what God wants to accomplish within a worship service. A song of lament is not appropriate, for instance, if we have been called upon to praise God!

The diverse range of songs for worship compares to the diversity of the prayers we are told to 'pray always in *all manner* of prayer and supplication in the Spirit' (Ephesians 6:18). Moreover, we should recall that an outworking of being filled with the Spirit is 'speaking to yourselves in psalms and hymns and spiritual songs, singing and making melody in your heart to the Lord' (Ephesians 5:19).

Perhaps equally, or even more dangerous, are songs tagged with the "Christian" label which can end up turning a man's heart further from the Truth of God's word. These cleverly written, pleasing to the ear, and adequately sentimental songs do not pass muster when compared with what God is saying to us in His word. The problem, though, is that few Christians appear to distinguish the difference between a song that is full of faith and one full of doubt and unbelief.

Some would argue that the scriptural accuracy of the songs we choose to sing or even what song is appropriate at any given time does not matter as "God understands what I mean". Well, He does understand; He promised to answer even before we call (Isaiah 65:24). God's nature revealed in the Holy Scriptures contradicts the notion that His understanding somehow absolves us of the requirement to be specific in our prayers, petitions and even in the songs that we choose to sing.

God has revealed Himself as being determined and specific in His dealings with mankind; indeed, from creation we can see that there are no mistakes, errors, or miscalculations with Him. The Bible describes God as 'the Father of lights in whom there is no variableness or shadow of turning'. The NET Bible translation renders it in this way:

> *'all generous giving and every perfect gift is from above, coming down from the Father of lights, with whom there is no variation or the slightest hint of change' (James 1:17).*

There is not the slightest hint of change in God. Whatever He has said, He will bring to pass. This does not take anything away from the mercy He so lavishly gives, both to those who know Him and those who are yet to know Him as He truly is. God IS merciful; however, He also wants us to grow spiritually. Those who stubbornly refuse to grow in the knowledge of God do themselves and, potentially others, a great disservice. To obstinately refrain from searching the scriptures for the ways He has prescribed for seeking His face, or even "just" singing His praise, is to knowingly give in to the schemes of the devil whose ultimate goal is to '...steal, kill and destroy.' (John 10:10). The preceding statement may at first appear to be an exaggeration, but when we consider the consequences of our actions (or in this case, our inaction); we may be forced to agree. God says, "My people perish for lack of knowledge".

When we consider the songs we sing as a vehicle to draw our hearts, minds and bodies towards God, we must look to His Word for His instruction by the inspiration of His Holy Spirit.

His word is Spirit and Life

In Deuteronomy, we read about how God instructed Moses to teach the Israelites a song:

> *'Now therefore write this song and teach it to the people of Israel. Put it in their mouths, that this song may be a witness for me against the people of Israel.' (Deuteronomy 31:19)*

This song is then recorded in the next chapter. We should note that God asked for this "witness" to be recorded in the form of a song that His people would sing to remember what He had foretold – both Israel's apostasy and His redemption plan.

After Moses had finished speaking the words of this God-given song to Israel, he made an important observation:

> *"Take to heart all the words by which I am warning you today, that you may command them to your children, that they may be careful to do all the words of this law. For it is no empty word for you, but your very life, and by this word you shall live long in the land that you are going over the Jordan to possess." (Deuteronomy 32:46, 47 ESV)*

In verse 47; the Word from God, given as a song, is described as "...your very life." Jesus said in John 6:63,

> *'...the words that I speak unto you, they are spirit and they are life.'*

This highlights how every worship songwriter should approach their song-writing. The inherent power of your position as a worship songwriter should make you take that gift seriously.

Spend time waiting on the Holy Spirit and in the Word, to ensure that the songs are not just pleasing to the ears but are scripturally sound, accurate, and infused with the power of the Holy Spirit. As we saw with the song of Moses, the songs we sing in Church have a main role in shaping our theology! Songs written by the inspiration of the Holy Spirit, backed by a sound knowledge and understanding of the scriptures will promote a genuine love for the Word of God, and also has the potential to change contrary circumstances in the lives of the singers, as long as it is mixed with faith. God's Word is living and active; therefore, whether spoken or sung, when it is mixed with faith, its ability to positively affect any negative situations remains. The importance of viewing the word of God we read, study, hear or indeed sing, from a position of faith, is highlighted in the book of Hebrews, chapter 4: 2

> *"for we also are having good news proclaimed, even as they, but the word heard did not profit them, not being mixed with faith in those who heard" (YLT)*

This passage is following on from the preceding chapter, where the writer of the book of Hebrews recounts God's anger against the children of Israel who wandered in the wilderness for forty years. The generation of Israelites that left Egypt for the Promised Land perished in the wilderness because they did not take God at His word. They saw the miracles He performed, heard all His great and precious promises, yet disobeyed Him again and again, because they did not truly believe. Lack of belief in God's power and promises made them long for the delicacies of Egypt (see Exodus 16:3, Numbers 11:5) and eventually led them to apostasy as they completely turned their back on God and created a "god" for themselves! (Exodus 32:1) No matter how scripturally accurate our songs are, if we do not truly believe what we are singing, and do not trust that God has done what He said He has done, we might as well not bother.

Moreover, if we are not prepared to follow our declarations of faith with corresponding action; that "faith" is dead! We are merely playing games!

God's Word is the "vehicle" of His power

The Word of God is the carrier of His power and all Christians must understand this. Within that Word is His power to accomplish what He has said. Several scriptural passages confirm this statement ,including John 6:63, Hebrews 1:3, Isaiah 55:11, and even Genesis 1:3.

In the book of Genesis, right at the dawn of time; we are told that though the earth was without any form, and the Spirit of God was hovering over the face of that indistinct void, things did not begin to happen until "God said". Nothing happened until His Word came forth.

There is little difference between speaking the word and singing it. What is more important is that we are not just going through the motions, reciting vain repetitions, but we truly believe what we are saying with our hearts and are ready to confirm what we believe by the actions we take. "Giving voice" to God's Word by singing it means we are employing that same power in His word to effect changes in our world. We have the confidence therefore, to go forth and preach, sing to, and about, God everywhere, assured that the Lord will work with us and confirm His word with signs following (See Mark 16:20). We are able to make declarations, pronounce blessings, prophesy, and repent of wrong-doing, just by our songs which have been inspired by the Holy Spirit. We must however, appreciate the increased tendency to resort to vain repetitions when singing rather than speaking God's word. There is a risk of easily being tempted to sing or speak words which may appear full of faith, but, because our hearts are not in what we are doing, are hollow and empty. As believers, we should shun distractions so that we can engage our hearts and minds in worship. Moreover, to be effective Ambassadors of God's Kingdom, we need to accept that there is a price to pay. Although Jesus said we should come to Him with our burdens so He might give us rest; He also said we should take up His yoke and burdens. His yoke, though easy, and burdens though light, are yokes and burdens just the same (Matthew 11:28–30).

There is a cost to walking in the fullness of God's assignment. When Jesus walked the Earth, He took the time to wait on His God given assignment. Several accounts in the Gospels tell us that He withdrew Himself from everyone else, so He could pray and fellowship with the Father (see Luke 5:16, Matthew 14:23, Mark 1:35).

Our desire as worshippers and songwriters should be to sing and write songs which place God at the centre. These are songs which build faith in us and in so doing, change us and transform our circumstances from one level of glory to the next. These will all be accomplished while increasing our knowledge of who God is, what He has done, and what He will do.

Furthermore, as the body of Christ, we can and should play our part by rejecting the messages of songs touted as songs for worship which are liable to spread error within the body. Pastors especially, should examine those songs which are being used for congregational worship. Sadly, we appear to be losing, at least in the mainstream of Christian music, the art of putting scriptures to music verbatim. This is an aspect of congregational worship which we should seek to actively cultivate. We are encouraged in the scriptures:

> *'Let the word of Christ dwell in you richly, teaching and admonishing one another in all wisdom, singing psalms and hymns and spiritual songs, with thankfulness in your hearts to God.' (Colossians 3: 16 ESV)*

This verse suggests that we teach one another through singing, identifying the preferred song content as well as the appropriate attitude of the heart, that is, thankfulness.

On a personal note, I remember how elated I felt as a young Christian, whenever I was reading my Bible and came across words from a song I had previously learnt. My first experiences of hiding God's word in my heart came from singing songs of worship in Christian meetings, which I later discovered in my Bible. I doubt that I am unique in this way, but I do still remember and sing some of these songs when faced with situations where I need the word of faith to come alive within me.

A further advantage of singing faith-filled, God's word filled songs is that they present a quick and pleasant way to commit God's Word into our hearts and minds. As a result, faith rises within us as we sing His word back to Him!

Dear Songwriter, does the prospect of impacting someone's life while glorifying God with your ability to write great songs fill you with excitement?

The entire man – spirit soul and body

In the book of Romans, we are told not to walk after the flesh, but according to the spirit. This means that we ought to walk according to the dictates of our spirits rather than our carnal selves – Romans 8:4. This is of course diametrically opposed to popular modern culture which says in essence: "do whatever makes you (your flesh) happy".

Every born-again child of God has become a brand new creation. This newness of life is, obviously not in our physical bodies, as there is no evident transformation in our physical appearance, neither do we physically become babies all over again! That we have become a new creation is not immediately evident in our personalities – our minds, our will and our emotions. It is our spirits which are reborn, the internal part of us, uniquely fashioned in God's image and has been endowed with the inherent ability to communicate with our Heavenly Father. Our priority as Christians should always be to seek to train our minds (an integral part of our souls) to listen to the voice of our spirits rather than the dictates of our flesh; remembering that our spirit is the only part of us with the ability to communicate with God – God is Spirit!

> *'Do not be conformed to this world, but be transformed by the renewal of your mind, that by testing you may discern what is the will of God, what is good and acceptable and perfect.' (Romans 12:2 ESV)*

The scriptures warn us to be transformed by renewing our minds. Pampering the flesh should not be our priority. This is not to suggest that the other parts of our being, (soul and body) are in any way irrelevant; rather, the case is being made here to give each part its rightful position and priority. When, as songwriters, we write according to our whims, sentiments, or preconceived notions and ideas which find no actual basis in scripture; we run the risk of creating songs which though may be pleasing to the ear (pleasing to the flesh), capable of drawing the "strings" of our emotions (soulish), would eventually promote the spread of error within the Body of Christ. Songs such as these would at best leave us on an emotional high with no real substance, or at their worst, promote the spread of error in the Body of Christ. Songs not substantiated by the word of God potentially spread error by propagating ideas which though sound logical and sentimental, do not stand up to scrutiny when compared with what the scriptures say.

More often than not, the type of error described here is not something that can be identified "from a mile off". Remember, the Bible says that even Satan is transformed into an "Angel of Light". It is often a subtle erosion of the truth or a slight modification of the truth. Consider the crafty way the serpent deceived the woman at the beginning, by deliberately confusing her, asking: "Did God actually say, 'you shall not eat of any tree in the garden'?" (Genesis 3:1 ESV). This was a calculated attempt to cause the woman to doubt God's giving nature. The serpent was subtly saying; God must be rather wicked; do you mean to say that this God would create all these beautiful trees laden with succulent fruit and then tell you not to enjoy it? The woman (later known as Eve) responded in confusion. Her confusion is apparent because she added to what God had commanded. She said, "but God said, you shall not eat of the fruit of the tree that is in the midst of the garden, ***neither shall you touch it, lest you die***" (emphasis mine). Eve added to God's command, making optional, what God had said would be certain! According to God's command, death was a certainty once man ate the fruit of the tree of the knowledge of good and evil. It was not a suggestion, neither was it a probability. Notice that the devil used this same tactic when he tempted the Lord Jesus Christ in the wilderness – questioning the express will of Jehovah. However, where the first Adam failed and gave in to the wiles of Satan, the last Adam, (Jesus Christ), rather than get into a discussion with the tempter, defeated him by the weapon of the Word of God.

That Christians should be fully acquainted with the word of God cannot be overemphasised. This is the only offensive weapon we have in our arsenal (see Ephesians 6:10–17). Permitting scriptural truth alone in the songs we write, or even setting melodies to actual scriptures where appropriate, to help new Christians to commit God's Word to memory is something we should aspire towards.

While it is important to aim to help develop the spirits of the hearers of the songs we write, we are not advocating songs lacking in creativity and imagination, just as long as they are true to scripture! There has been an undeniable explosion of creativity in the popular worship songs today. To draw people in, especially the younger generation, we must ensure that we are not offering an inferior product! The word of caution here is to alert our minds to what is of paramount importance, so that the true message of the gospel of Jesus Christ is not lost in our bid to stay relevant to society in general and the younger generation in particular.

Exegesis or Eisegesis – Rightly dividing the Word of Truth

> *'Do your best to present yourself to God as one approved, a worker who has no need to be ashamed, rightly handling the word of truth.' (2 Timothy 2:15 ESV)*

We understand from the Bible that our worship must be "in spirit" and "in truth". The songs we sing, though possessing the potential to instruct in the word of truth, can equally encourage the spread of error. The fact that there is a way to handle the word of truth correctly indicates that there is also a wrong way to do so. Therefore, if we are to worship our Father the way He dictates, we must ensure that we are worshipping Him based on the truth He has revealed to us through His written word. This once again highlights the importance of studying God's word.

I feel the need to re-emphasise here, the importance that God places on His revealed word. God has faithfully preserved His word for us – against all odds, and for generations. Jesus said; "Heaven and earth shall pass away, but my words shall not pass away." (Matthew 24:35). If all the Earth, as well as the Heavens as we know them will be done away with, we ought to pay attention to the one thing which will survive! There is a depth to the word of God which we can never grasp until we begin to pay due attention to it!

In delving into the word of God, we must pay attention to the differences between searching out what the Holy Spirit was saying through the human author of any passage of scripture, and, approaching the scriptures with our preconceived ideas of what we want to say and then attempt to "shoe horn" that interpretation to a particular passage. We must be aware that we live in a different dispensation from the old Covenant. There are major differences between Old Covenant worship and New Covenant worship.

To drive our point home, we will take a quick look at some of the subtle ways that our word choices in song writing can misguidedly shape the theology of a body of believers. We will be looking at specific songs or themes explored in some of the songs used for congregational worship in many Churches today.

First, consider those songs which urge the Holy Spirit to "come and meet us" which are continually being written and sung in churches everywhere, with great expectations of God's manifest presence. These songs appear to neglect all the assurances we have been given that God is indeed with us! He lives in us – Romans 8:11, Christ is in us; the hope of glory (Colossians 1:27), He promised to never leave nor forsake us. He is with us always and has given us His solemn promise that He is our "ever present God".

Perhaps it is appropriate for those yet to experience the Baptism of the Holy Spirit to call on God in this way for an outpouring of His Spirit; as this baptism does differ extensively from the indwelling which occurs at the moment we are born again. However, those who have received this baptism should instead seize every opportunity to thank God for this precious gift, thanking Him for the grace to fulfill the purpose for which the gift was given!

Revelation 3:20 paints a beautiful picture of the fellowship our Lord desires to have with His people:

> *"Behold, I stand at the door and knock. If anyone hears my voice and opens the door, I will come in to him and eat with him, and he with Me."*

Our confidence should be in His promises rather than in how we feel. We may not "feel" the presence of God with us, but we should rest on His word which He has given. I do not wish to downplay the fact that as children of God, we have access to both the indwelling of the Holy Spirit (which we receive when we are born again), the Baptism of the Holy Spirit, as well as the fact that we are encouraged to be "continually filled with the Spirit". (Ephesians 5:18–21)

> *"And be not drunk with wine, wherein is excess; but be filled with the Spirit; speaking to yourselves in psalms and hymns and spiritual songs, singing and making melody in your heart to the Lord; giving thanks always for all things unto God and the Father in the name of our Lord Jesus Christ; submitting yourselves one to another in the fear of God."*

Various Bible scholars agree that "be filled with the Spirit" is more properly rendered as "be *continually* filled with the Spirit"; as it was written in a present continuous tense rather than past tense. The interesting thing about these verses which the songs begging for the Holy Spirit to "come and fill us anew" do not take into consideration is that we are immediately told ***how*** to be continually filled:

- By speaking to one another in psalms and hymns and spiritual songs
- By singing and making melody in our hearts to the Lord
- By giving thanks always for all things unto God and the Father in the Name of our Lord Jesus Christ
- By submitting ourselves to one another in the fear of God.

Some have used the account in Acts 4:31 to justify the widespread practice of actively asking the Holy Spirit to fill us anew, to fill us afresh, be poured out on us etc. If we consider the occurrence in context, we see that these believers, (the same ones who had been previously filled on the day of Pentecost) were not seeking for the Holy Spirit to fill them afresh! Instead, they worshipped God, reminded Him (and themselves) of His promise through David, and prayed for boldness to continue their assignment!

When we acknowledge God's presence (in the person of the Holy Spirit), in our lives, we become more aware of His presence!

The type of songs we have been exploring are those which were written specifically as songs for worship; either as part of a congregational worship service or those we sing to God in worship and adoration in our private time with Him. There are also songs containing instructions, exhortations, encouragement etc. which though may not be appropriate for congregational worship, are nevertheless of great value in building up the Body of Christ. We have previously identified that some worship songs, because of their subject matter or the way they have been arranged, lend themselves more to being sung in private than in a congregational setting. There are also those tagged with the Christian label which appear to have been written and performed more for their entertainment value than anything else. However, the lines between these types of songs and those introduced for congregational worship are getting increasingly blurred.

The Christian songs written and or performed more for their "entertainment value" as suggested here, tend to focus more on the vocal prowess of the soloists and backing vocalists, the level of skill of the musicians, how cleverly the songs were arranged and how closely they match the current trends in the world of secular music. They are usually less focused on scriptural accuracy and do not appear to be concerned with how easy it is for the listener to retain the melody in their hearts, so they can use them in their private time of worship. Moreover, too many of these songs are full of complaints, grumbling and explore human feelings and emotions and basically anything else than actual adoration of the One we are supposed to be worshipping!

Many songs paraded for congregational worship are man-centred, rather than God-centred and place undue emphasis on where we see ourselves, the way we see ourselves, what we want Him to do for us – essentially, they gratify the flesh, elicit strong emotional responses and encourage a passive approach to Christianity. Additionally, large numbers of the songs touted as "Christian" display such a blatant disregard for the legacy of Scripture and the fact that we already have "everything that pertains to life and godliness"! Instead of begging God for what He has already made available to us, we should be developing our faith in order to fully walk in the fullness of what Jesus Christ has already purchased for us. Rather than "waiting for God to move"; we ought to realise that He is actually waiting for us to step out in faith! In fact, we are told that the entire creation of God is waiting with eager longing for the revealing of the sons of God.

Those songs that encourage a passive Christian experience are particularly dangerous because they essentially prevent the child of God from embracing some of the most fundamental truths revealed in scriptures:

The scriptures say that the communication of our faith is made effective when we acknowledge what is (already) in us in Christ Jesus (see Philemon 1:6). We are already blessed with every spiritual blessing in the heavenly places in Christ Jesus (Ephesians 1:3). Jesus Christ is right now, seated at the right hand of God in the heavenly places, far above all rule and authority and power and dominion, and above every name that is named, not only in this age but also in the one to come. Not only that, but God raised us with Christ and made us sit together in heavenly places with Him! (Ephesians 1:20, 21; 2:6)

When we do not appreciate the truth of our positioning in Christ, we are forced to take the posture of begging for crumbs at the table He has prepared for us!

Sadly, the type of songs to which I refer, encourage this passive posture, where we ask, plead, beg and bargain with God to come and do again, what He has already accomplished in Christ! Too many songs intended for worship are written from a place of need and lack, rather than from the reality of all that Christ has purchased for us by His blood.
Another example I would like to give here, in my opinion, typifies those songs which have enough "truth" in them as to inoculate the hearer against the Truth! The first three lines of the song I have in mind goes thus:

> *"You are good; You are good, when there is nothing good in me..."*

Now, this looks innocent enough and was undoubtedly written with the best intentions; until we begin to delve into the treasury of Scripture. The first part of Romans 7:18 says unequivocally; "For I know that nothing good dwells in me..." and if we stopped there, then that line in the song would be completely correct! However, that verse goes on to qualify the specific part of the makeup of man to which it refers – is it his spirit, his soul or his body? The complete verse states: "for I know that nothing good dwells in me, that is, in my flesh", signifying that nothing good dwells in his flesh; in his body – his "carnal self".
After throwing up his hands in apparent defeat at the fact that he has the desire to do what is right, but not the ability to carry it out (Romans 7:21), in the very next chapter, the Apostle Paul (remember, he is writing by the inspiration of the Holy Spirit) proffers the solution!
"There is therefore now no condemnation to them which are in Christ Jesus, *who walk not after the flesh, but after the Spirit.*" (Romans 8:1)

> *"That the righteousness of the law might be fulfilled in us, who walk not after the flesh, but after the Spirit. For they that*

> *are after the flesh do mind the things of the flesh; but they that are after the Spirit the things of the Spirit." (Romans 8:4, 5)*

In fact, most of the eighth chapter of the book of Romans is dedicated to convincing us of the merits to be found in walking in the Spirit, as well as the consequences of living according to the dictates of the flesh. Why then, would I want to sing about my flesh, (albeit in contrast to God), when I am supposed to be acknowledging the good in me? We must not forget that the songs we sing represent a particularly potent form of meditation. What we meditate upon, according to the scriptures, is what we become; – "as he thinketh in his heart, so is he". (Proverbs 23:7)
This third example is included to illustrate the confusion between Old Testament history and New Covenant truths.

> *"Take me past the outer courts, into the holy place, past the brazen altar, Lord; I want to see your face..."*

This song, complete with its beautiful melody and stirring lyrics, nevertheless neglects the fact that "the veil has been torn in two"; we no longer have to "go past the brazen altar" in order to get an audience with the God of the heavens and the Earth. No, rather than being led timidly and passively into God's presence, in the New covenant; because of Jesus' finished work on the cross at Calvary, we are told to approach God's throne, directly and boldly!
A final example would be those songs which are increasingly cropping up these days. These are songs that have no discernible scriptural basis or foundations, except that they sound vaguely like they belong in the Bible and are sufficiently emotive and sentimental in the message they proclaim:

> *"If grace is an ocean, we're all sinking, so heaven meets earth like a sloppy wet kiss and my heart turns violently inside of my chest..."*

Where to begin with this one? I realise that this is just a small part of the song, but the imagery it produces in the mind is just so surreal. Nonetheless, this particular song became extremely popular and many attest to the intense emotions they feel when the song is played or when they are singing it during corporate worship. The question we might want to ask though, is whether any intense emotional reactions to this song serve as enough validation of what the song represents?

Unfortunately, these songs are finding their way into our Churches, unquestioned, where they are increasingly being heralded as great songs of worship. The inclusion of "novices", rather than proven disciples – (see 1 Timothy 3:6) as worship leaders because of their evident talents may account for this apparent lack of discernment. Novices mentioned here do not refer to recent converts alone, but also those who are still "spiritual babies". This is not a function of how long we have been Christians for, but rather how much we have grown in our walk with God and have become "skilful in the word of righteousness".

> *"For though by this time you ought to be teachers, you need someone to teach you again the basic principles of the oracles of God. You need milk, not solid food, for everyone who lives on milk is unskilled in the word of righteousness, since he is a child. But solid food is for the mature, for those who have their powers of discernment trained by constant practice to distinguish good from evil."(Hebrews 5:12 – 14 ESV)*

It has to be said though, not only novices could be caught in the web of confusion regarding the appropriate songs for worship. It is just as easy for a mature Christian to fall prey to actively promoting dubious songs for worship simply because they have either not paid enough attention or they have been deceived. Remember, Satan himself is transformed into an angel of light. There is only one reason for this; it is to enable him deceive as

many as he can! I daresay that those who write these songs are themselves victims of the deceitful wiles of the enemy.
Some Christian artistes have however been able to find a happy medium and niche for themselves, where they produce clean songs with godly principles which are equally as likely to be heard on secular radio as they are on Christian radio. These artistes are bucking the trends while proving that we do not need to compromise ourselves nor water down the message of the gospel in order to reach a wider audience.

A time for everything

We have already discussed the fact that we are to "enter into God's presence" with praise and thanksgiving! While I do not intend to define a specific guideline which our worship services should adhere to, we should stay in close communication with the Holy Spirit and remain aware of what we are doing while leading worship. When we are praising God, let us praise **Him**! That is not the time to be repenting, neither is it the time to be lamenting the ills of society! Of course, a time of exuberant praise could then, by the Holy Spirit's guidance, lead on to a time of repentance before God but let it be "as we are led" rather than "as we think". There is, after all, a time for every purpose under the heaven: "...a time to weep, and a time to laugh; a time to mourn and a time to dance;" (Ecclesiastes 3:4). If we think about the songs we sing or write as not just "songs" but potential carriers of God's power through His Word, perhaps then we would begin to pay the appropriate amount of attention to what we are doing and when. The Bible already tells us in 1 Peter 4:11;

> *"If any man speak, let him speak as the oracles of God; if any man minister, let him do it as of the ability which God giveth: that God in all things may be glorified through Jesus Christ, to whom be praise and dominion forever and ever. Amen."*

This tells us where our emphasis should be; placed solely on God who is the One on whom we are to depend rather than on our 'natural' ability. This is so that what we do is endued or saturated with God's power. Our skills, talents and natural ability are of little profit (in the eternal scheme of things) if we do not take the time to wait on the Lord for "power from on high." (See 1 Corinthians 2:4).

POINTS TO PONDER

---

1. What is the importance of developing skills and talents?
2. If you enjoy music, do you agree that there is a need to determine what is appropriate for you to listen to as a believer or are you deliberately not selective in what you listen to?
3. Why is it important to "rightly divide the word of truth"? Can you give some examples you have come across where some may have been "wrongly dividing" God's word?
4. How are you able to determine whether you have truly experienced God's manifest presence in a worship service? Was it because tears were welling up from your eyes for instance?
5. What is your yardstick for measuring how good a worship song is?
6. Have you ever considered whether a praise song you heard is true to scripture? Does this bother you at all or do you not think of scriptural accuracy at all?
7. In your opinion, how important is scriptural accuracy in the songs of praise and worship you sing?

CHAPTER 6:

Play skilfully – Wanted; a worship band.

Sing unto Him a new song; play skilfully with a loud noise (Psalm 33:3)

The book of Job, which many Biblical scholars regard as a record of things that happened long before the birth of Moses, describes the rejoicing that took place in Heaven when God created the Earth, saying:

> *"...where were you when I laid the foundation of the earth? Tell Me if you have understanding. When the morning stars sang together, and all the sons of God (angels) shouted for joy!"*
>
> *(Job 38:4, 7 ESV)*

This verse gives us a glimpse into some of what goes on in heaven – joyous shouting! It is no wonder therefore that the entire Bible is full of words of encouragement to rejoice!

Congregational worship in the Old Testament always included the playing of musical instruments. The first song recorded in the Bible is the song of Moses in Exodus 15. The children of Israel sang this song when they were delivered from the hands of Pharaoh. God parted the Red Sea so His people could walk across on dry land then He caused the waters to come back over the Egyptians who had been pursuing them. (Exodus 14;21–30). This miraculous victory was cause for great rejoicing in the camp of the Israelites, and we read:

> *"Miriam the prophetess, the sister of Aaron, took a timbrel in her hand; and all the women went out after her with timbrels and with dances."*

Miriam took on the role of a worship leader, leading all the women who followed her with their own timbrels and dances.

Playing instruments during worship

There may have been other songs prior to Miriam's song since we are introduced to Jubal, one of the descendants of Cain in the book of Genesis. Jubal was described as: "the father of all such as handle the harp and organ". (Genesis 4:21). Not much else is said about Jubal, but we can deduce he came from a race of ungodly people as he was a direct descendant of an unrepentant Cain whom God had cursed.

The unfortunate association between the "ungodly" and playing of musical instruments may have helped form the opinion of many who eschew the use of musical instruments in congregational worship, particularly when combined with the argument that the application of musical instruments in worship is not directly mentioned in the New Testament.

Paradoxically, many of these same people apparently have no problems with secular music and instrumentation; retaining their aversion to instrumental music for worship music only; a baffling reaction indeed!

There is no doubt instrumental music has been used historically for promoting innumerable satanic devices, including actual "demon worship". Music is even today, still being used to help people lose their inhibitions in a bid to make their will more pliable. The loss of inhibitions promotes a lack of restraint, ultimately leading to promiscuous and depraved behaviour.

We understand from the scriptures that our enemy, Satan, does not create anything from scratch, and is limited to perverting those things which have been created. Therefore, he continues a systematic perversion of the beautiful God-designed gift of music.

The consequence of Satan's onslaught against music is evident in the global entertainment industry today. Nevertheless, though the Devil and his cohorts have made such an inroad into the content, performance, and dissemination of music, we do not have enough grounds to hand this wonderful gift from God to his complete control. Every good and perfect gift comes from above (James 1:17) and when we understand that God gave man dominion over the Earth in its entirety, we can conclude that Music is one of those things that He would have man regain dominion over. This will in turn ensure that Music is then reconciled to its original purpose; which is to glorify God!

When we see someone accomplished as a musician, particularly when they are very young, we call them a "gifted person" or a prodigy. Where does that "gift" come from? The scriptures tell us that every good gift comes from God the Father of lights and that the devil does not have the ability to create anything. All he can do is attempt to pervert whatever he can, making counterfeits of the original creation. The devil perverts the gift of music as much as he can, as he seeks to inspire those obviously gifted by God to produce material which appear to have come directly from the throes of hell itself as indicated by the dark, depressing, and often depraved content they produce!

Perverted music as described above may be viewed as extreme examples of instrumental music which has not been submitted to God; there is undoubtedly a lot of music produced which though cannot be labelled Christian, do promote positive messages. It is difficult to argue however with the fact that popular culture in the 21st Century is normalising these perversions and making them increasingly mainstream. Additionally, huge sums of money have been dedicated to the study of the influence of music on our purchasing patterns in retail environments. This means that each time we walk into a retail shop, our subconscious is arrested by canned music from public address systems which have been designed specifically to keep us in those shops for much longer than intended so that we consequently spend more than we may have originally been prepared to.

Most people will readily admit that playing the appropriate type of music at the right time can, and does produce a calming effect on frayed nerves. This is the effect David's playing of the harp had on Saul when a spirit of depression came upon him:

> *"Saul sent to Jesse, saying, "Let David now stand before me, for he has found favour in my sight." And it came to pass, when the evil spirit from God was upon Saul, that David took an harp, and played with his hand: so Saul was refreshed, and was well, and the evil spirit departed from him."(1 Samuel 16: 22-23)*

A copious amount of money is being spent on scientific research into subliminal and supraliminal messages deliberately sent to our subconscious to elicit a particular response. This fact alone should be enough to make us seriously consider and evaluate what we are listening to.

The ability to create and also enjoy or appreciate music, the aroma of a fine fragrance, the beauty of a work of art, the texture of fine fabric, the taste of some delicacy are all gifts from God our Father who gives us all things richly to enjoy:

> *"...charge them that are rich in this world, that they be not high-minded, nor trust in uncertain riches, but in the living*

> *God, who giveth us richly all things to enjoy;" (1 Timothy 6:17).*

God the Father, in a demonstration of His love towards us, gave us these gifts so that we can enjoy the world He created for us. Indeed our Lord Jesus Christ said in John 10:10 that 'I am come that they might have life, and that they might have it more abundantly'! It is important to remember though, that our "enjoyment" of this world is predicated on the fact that we were created to give pleasure to our God. (See Revelation 4:11).
1 Corinthians 10:31 and Colossians 3:17 tell us that whatever we do should be to the glory of God. These verses provide a solid foundation upon which we can build our daily lives. We must determine to shun pure ambition, and focus instead on discovering the will of God and then act upon it.
The ongoing debate about whether it is appropriate to play musical instruments as part of our congregational worship centres around the opinions of those who argue that there is no specific instruction in the New Testament that requires the use of musical instruments. I however, do not believe that there is anything intrinsically wrong with playing musical instruments within the framework of a worship service. Music can, and does, enhance our worship, as long as we are careful not to depend too heavily on instrumental music. Imagine for instance, a time of loud exuberant praise quenched abruptly because the drummer broke his last drumstick!

> *"Let the high praises of God be in their mouth and a two-edged sword in their hand; to execute vengeance upon the heathen, and punishments upon the people..." (Psalm 149:6, 7)*

High praise referred to here is not just talking about loud praise, though loud praise is not precluded. When we are mindful that our praise is a weapon of warfare and we are truly in the process of putting the enemy to flight with our praise, it would be a great shame to lose that momentum in praise warfare because something happened to the musical instruments at just the wrong time. Rather than suddenly go quiet because the "music" is no longer booming and we are not sure what exactly is happening at the time; we should allow our voices, in tandem with our hearts, take over in declaring the praises of our God and King!

Play skilfully:

O LORD our Lord, how excellent is Your Name in all the earth! (Psalm 8:9)
There is an aspect of God's character that speaks of His excellence. He did create everything perfectly at the beginning of time. God gave every one of us gifts and talents which He expects us to "trade with" upon this earth. In the Old Testament, right from when He gave the precise specifications for the Ark to Noah, we see that God does not believe in half-measures, not even in the design of an ark which was to be a temporary home for a man, his family, and a whole lot of animals!
The calling of Bezalel the son of Uri of the tribe of Judah in Exodus 31 further illustrates the attention that God gives to details. All the articles for corporate worship were to be constructed carefully to the precise specifications given by God Himself!

> *'...See, I have called by name Bezalel the son of Uri, the son of Hur, of the tribe of Judah: And I have filled him with the spirit of God, in wisdom, and in understanding, and in knowledge, and in all manner of workmanship, To devise cunning works, to work in gold, and in silver, and in brass, And in cutting of stones, to set them, and in carving of timber, to work in all manner of workmanship. And I, behold, I have given with him Aholiab, the son of Ahisamach, of the tribe of Dan: and in the hearts of all that are wise hearted I have put wisdom, that they may make all that I have commanded thee;'(Exodus 31:1-6)*

This passage of scripture is relevant to our study as it highlights the fact that God specifically gifted Bezalel to carry out this task. God gave him a gift which he would have not only identified but also developed over the years. Notice that God put wisdom "in the hearts of all that are wise hearted". This suggests that these individuals played a specific part in placing themselves in position to receive that wisdom. Most of the other translations equally indicate that God placed wisdom into the hearts of those who were already skilled. The importance of developing skill, trading with the talents God gives to us cannot be overemphasised. While this applies to virtually every sphere of life, it is particularly relevant in the music ministry. 1 Corinthians 14:8 declares, "...if the trumpet give an uncertain sound, who shall prepare himself to the battle?" The value of the trumpet as a means of rallying the troops is completely lost if the notes played on it are not clear and precise. Anyone who has been part of a worship service where discordant notes were played on musical instruments would readily testify to the truth of the statement made in 1 Corinthians 14:8!

Once again, looking at the calling of Bezalel in the passage above, notice that in the 6th verse, God placed wisdom in "...the hearts of all that were wise-hearted". This wisdom was to enable them to properly execute their God-given assignment so they could make all the articles for worship which God had commanded Moses to make.

It is highly improbable, in light of scripture, for God to give you a gift without also placing a calling upon that gift! Now, this does not mean that everyone would answer that call; moreover, it is not necessarily everyone God calls that He chooses for a particular assignment. (See Matthew 22:14).

Some Christians erroneously believe that because God is All-knowing and All-powerful, if He wants them to have something, they will get it. They think that if God has placed a calling on their lives, then He will make them answer it, or, if God wants something to happen on the earth, He will do it. This flawed thinking must be dispelled once and for all. Psalm 115:16 reminds us of what took place right at the beginning of time, declaring: “The heaven, even the heavens, are the LORD'S: but the earth hath He given to the children of men”. You and I have been given a direct mandate from God to have dominion over the earth and subdue it. In the commissioning of Adam and Eve; God, in telling them to be fruitful, multiply and replenish the earth and have dominion over it, was establishing mankind to become co-creators with Him!

The calling of Daniel and his friends further illustrates the requirement for those who would be used by God to develop their gifting, to add skills to their talents. Raw talent is never enough!

> *“Then the king commanded Ashpenaz, his chief eunuch, to bring some of the people of Israel, both of the royal family and of the nobility, youth without blemish, of good appearance and skilful in all wisdom, endowed with knowledge, understanding learning, and competent to stand in the king's palace, and to teach them the literature and language of the Chaldeans.” (Daniel 1:3, 4. ESV)*

This was the beginning of Daniel's life in the kingdom of Babylon. He was taken, along with many others, from their home to Babylon. Then he was chosen because of his gifting. The first six chapters of the book of Daniel clearly demonstrate the development of character in the man Daniel who shunned the threats of terrible consequences to himself in order to fully obey God. So, Daniel was no doubt a gifted man, but he also developed skills and character so that his gift was continually called upon.

Now someone may wonder, “What do the lives of men like Daniel or Bezalel have to do with worship”?

Well, first, we need to remember that our lives, our existence depends on the mercy of God. We have been encouraged to

present our bodies a living sacrifice so that, everything we do, is to the glory of God! Therefore, whether we develop our gifts and talents to such an extent as to be deemed worthy to fashion the first physical “dwelling place” for God on earth; or we develop them enough to take us to the second highest position of honour in our land of captivity; as long as we are motivated by a desire to serve God, obey Him and bring glory to His Name; we are engaged in worship! We need to understand that we always have a choice in the matter, we can choose whether to obey God's directives or not, and He does not enforce His will on us. We should remember though, that our choices and actions have consequences. This is why God would say in Deuteronomy 30:19 that He set before us one of two choices, life or death. While He advises us to “choose life”, we are also “free” to choose death if we so desire. The choice is ours to make! What most of us do not enjoy is the fact that it takes faith to obey God. We are told to start, to begin what we have been called to do, but while He gives us a vision of the end result, He never gives a complete blueprint of what He is calling us to do, because He wants us to trust in Him (and not in our own selves or abilities).
We each have our own part to play, our own responsibility to ensure that we are indeed “...a vessel unto honour, sanctified, and meet for the Master's use.” (2 Timothy 2:21)

Preparation; a key to success:

There is always a time of preparation before the call of God becomes manifest or evident in anyone's life.
David, the last son of his father Jesse had spent a good part of his youth being prepared while he was in the desert, looking after his father's sheep. This was a man who took the time to hone in his skills as a harp player, and become as skilled at this as to have been invited into king Saul's palace to play the harp for him.

Though this is not expressly recorded in the Bible, what we know about David tells us that he had also developed a close relationship with God. David knew his God and was able to do exploits for Him. David, having "practised" on the lion and the bear which came after the flock he tended in the desert, was fully prepared and had great confidence in God such that he was able to boldly approach the giant Goliath who had been threatening God's people.

In the same vein, those who believe they have a call of God on their lives should take appropriate time to "wait on their ministry". There is a need to take the time to prepare to answer that call. The preparation time must involve a deliberate and sustained time of developing our "spiritual muscles"; studying the word of God, and fellowshipping with the Holy Spirit. This would help us to learn to discern His voice in the midst of the multitude of contradicting voices and distractions. It is important to observe that this is a lifelong undertaking, rather than something we do in the short term only. Jesus said; "My sheep hear my voice and I know them and they follow Me" (John 10:27). This comes about only through regular interaction and not fleeting encounters.

Who needs a "worship team"?

In order to adequately tackle the question of whether a worship team, worship leader or worship band is necessary or not in these "modern" times, it is helpful to look at the foundations established in the scriptures.

First, we see how God separated the sons of Levi from the rest of the children of Israel – separated them unto Himself as a tribe of priests. Every priest was to come from the tribe of Levi only, although not every Levite was a priest. Those who were not priests were given the work of looking after the Tabernacle and its furnishings.

This is a story of God's redeeming grace as prior to this, Levi and his descendants had previously been cursed by their father for their wickedness in exacting revenge on their sister's behalf (see Genesis 34, 49:5–7). Jacob (Israel) had pronounced that Levi's descendants would be dispersed all over Israel saying, "...I will divide them in Jacob, and scatter them in Israel". (Genesis 49:7). In providing a way of redemption for Levi, God in His mercy separated the tribe of Levi unto Himself. He did this such that even though they would not have an inheritance in Israel like the rest of their brethren, they would have the privilege of counting God Himself as their inheritance.

We understand that God always had a plan of redemption which meant that His people would no longer need an imperfect mediator. The sacrifices made by the Levitical priests could not cleanse sin, but would just cover the people's sins from the wrath of God! Now we have the "...one mediator between God and men, the man Christ Jesus" (1 Timothy 2:5). Hallelujah!

When Jesus Christ died on the cross and the veil that separated the Holy place from the Holy of Holies was torn in two, He cleared the way for everyone who had come to trust in His saving grace to be bold enough to approach God's presence. While before, only the high priest could do this though with trepidation, and under the real fear of death, because of Jesus' sacrifice on the cross, we who are now the people of God and called by His Name, have been made "kings and priests unto God..." (Revelations: 1:6).

We are now all part of the Royal Priesthood, a people set apart unto God, called to show forth the praises of Him who has called us out of darkness into His marvellous light! (1 Peter 2:9).

As we begin to think about a worship team, we cannot ignore the man David, the one the Almighty God called "...a man after My own heart". David, when he became king, commissioned and established most of the instruments and songs used, first in the Tabernacle, and later for the Temple services in Israel (after his son Solomon built the temple).

A study of the book of first Chronicles yields a great deal of information about musical instruments in worship as prescribed by David the king. He was the one to establish a "Church" choir (first a choir for the Tabernacle and later for Temple worship).

These musicians and singers were full time "employees" who were engaged in their work day and night! (1 Chronicles 9:33).

"David also ordered the Levite leaders to appoint a choir of Levites who were singers and musicians to sing joyful songs to the accompaniment of harps, lyres and cymbals." (1 Chronicles 15:16 NLT).

The musicians and singers were appointed first, because they were from the right tribe – the only tribe from which the priests could come, and also because they were known to be skilled at what they did. There were also specific Levites appointed to perform specific duties even within this team of Levite singers and musicians. This prescription of non-stop worship represents a type of what is going on in Heaven before the throne of God right now, as we read in the book of Revelation about the four living creatures who do not rest, but day and night, (without ceasing) they keep on saying "Holy, Holy, Holy, Lord God Almighty, who was and who is and who is to come" (see Revelations 4:8). There is music in Heaven right now and this is a fact which those who argue against the use of music in modern day Church worship refuse to either acknowledge or grasp!

A modern-day choir/worship team ought also to be established in order to first, minister unto the Lord God and then, to help the congregation in their own worship unto God. Temple and tabernacle music in the old testament was a lavish affair, no half measures here – in fact, in one instance, when David had become old and had made his son Solomon king over Israel in his stead, we are told of 4000 Levites "praising the LORD with the instruments which David made for giving praise" (see 1

Chronicles 23:1–5). Think about that for a moment. A 4000 strong choir of skilled singers and musicians! There was nothing quiet nor subdued, tentative, or reflective about those worship services.

Let us remember that our gifting alone is not enough to fulfill God's purpose in our lives. This applies in all spheres of life in general, as well as specifically in the area of leading worship as a musician or a singer. We have to add to that gifting, develop those raw talents and submit ourselves to God. We must also actively develop godly character. A godly character will help us retain the anointing of the Holy Spirit. The owner of the gift, who generously gave gifts to men, is looking out to ensure that we are using that gift effectively; that we are "trading" with the talents He gave to us. (See the Parable of the Talents – Matthew 25:14–30).

POINTS TO PONDER

1. Do we need a worship team or even a worship leader for our congregational services?
2. Are worship bands more of a hindrance than enhancers of congregational worship?
3. How do you think Church worship teams, where available, should prepare? What are your reasons?
4. How should members of such teams be chosen? Is there is a need for preparation as well as continuous study?
5. What do you think are the more important characteristics of a good worship team?

CHAPTER 7:

Praise or Performance

"And my speech and my preaching were not with persuasive words of human wisdom, but in demonstration of the Spirit and of power, that your faith should not be in the wisdom of men but in the power of God." (1 Corinthians 2: 4 -5 NKJV)

Declare, proclaim, and show forth! These are all terms identified with praise in the scriptures. We have previously established that praise is visible, audible and often loud and enthusiastic; concluding that if we purse our lips, though we may be inwardly worshipping God or even thinking worrisome thoughts, we are definitely not engaged in the act of praising God!

We also by now ought to have come to some understanding of the importance of developing and deploying our skills or "trading with our talents" in our determination to worship our Creator while encouraging others to do the same.

There is something we must keep at the back of our minds when we think about praise and worship, which applies particularly to worship leaders and musicians. Our God is a God of beauty and excellence; in fact, everything He does, He does very well. This attribute of His ought to be replicated in the lives of His children. We ought to, in everything that we do, strive for excellence – so that "men may see our good works and glorify God in heaven." There is no room for half-heartedness here. The conundrum the Christian faces is differentiating between pursuing excellence for self-gratification or in order to gain the respect of others; and pursuing excellence because you know that God deserves your best in everything you do. Considering things from a natural point of view, it seems that no matter how skilled, how talented someone is; you don't often have to look too far to find someone who is either equally or even more talented. The rise of social media connections all over the world is giving talented people the exposure they have lacked for a long time, often bestowing international prominence on those who may have lived their lives in total obscurity otherwise.

For a Christian, charged with the God given mandate to display His manifold wisdom to principalities and powers; having great natural abilities, skills and talents is of no significance if they are not infused with God's power. This is not to diminish the need to develop our skills in whatever it is we do, nor is the intention to discourage the pursuit of excellence! Our God is an excellent God; the works of His hands are great and marvellous. Therefore, those talents God gifts us with, He does expect us to develop. The onus is on us His children to acknowledge Him in all our ways so that He is the One directing our pathways, rather than our own vain ambition, a desire to please man, or to gain recognition and accolades from man.

The subtle yet important differences between seeking for God's approval or man's approval become evident in our response for example, when things don't go quite as well as we had originally envisaged. If we embark on what we believe is a God-inspired project and the end results are far from satisfactory, what is our response? Do we label ourselves failures and continually blame ourselves for falling short? Or do we in reverence toward God, take it to Him in prayer, thanking Him for the privilege of being able to serve Him? Would we lean on the power of His Holy Spirit to show us where we may have missed His promptings and ask that He would help us do better next time?

Here then, lies the difference between praise and performance. It stems from the motivation of our hearts, the thoughts that we conceive and dwell upon in our secret place, that part of us where no other person has ever been before. Who are we ultimately trying to impress? That we are thinking in terms of "impressing" someone already exposes our hidden thoughts. We cannot impress God as He is, after all, the One who created us. It is in Him we live and move and have our being, so, there is no effective way we can impress Him! This means that, in seeking to impress, we are looking at those who are impressionable – other human beings like ourselves!

> *"For am I now seeking the approval of man, or of God? Or am I trying to please man? If I were still trying to please man, I would not be a servant of Christ." (Galatians 1:10 ESV)*

The interesting thing about getting our priorities straight, seeking God's approval rather than the approval of our fellow man, is that at the end of it all, we are likely to discover that we gained the respect of those who were looking on. This is the lot of those who determine to live as the servants of God; "When a man's ways please the Lord, He makes even his enemies to be at peace with him." (Proverbs 16:7)

If we are able to rid ourselves of the pressures of looking to impress other men, then we are ready to be mouldable instruments in the hands of our Maker!

The Call:

For everyone who is called by His Name, there is a divine assignment. This is true of every Christian, but whether we fulfil this assignment or not, is completely up to us. God gave man a free will, the ability and option to choose; He does not impose His will upon His children.

How then do we recognise this assignment? It is a process which begins when we identify the call of God upon our lives.
The first and ultimate call made to every individual, is the call to be saved. To receive salvation from the kingdom of darkness so that we may be translated into the Kingdom of God's dear Son! When we have answered that call, we receive the indwelling of the Holy Spirit (the Holy Spirit lives within us) and are then ready to receive the call to "ministry", that is, the call to serve. This is when we become aware of the gifts of the Holy Spirit, and receive His gifts as individuals which are for the profit of the entire Body of Christ:

> *"To each is given the manifestation of the Spirit for the common good. For to one is given through the Spirit the utterance of wisdom, and to another the utterance of knowledge according to the same Spirit, to another faith by the same Spirit, to another gifts of healing by the one Spirit, to another the working of miracles, to another prophecy, to another the ability to distinguish between spirits, to another various kinds of tongues, to another the interpretation of tongues. All these are empowered by one and the same Spirit, who apportions to each one individually as He wills." (1 Corinthians 12:7 - 11 ESV)*

Those who have received the saving grace of God immediately become members of the body of Christ, with each member having a specific part to play. This is much like the parts of a human body, each of which has a definitive function for the good of the entire body. Romans 12: 4–8 describes how we are to use these gifts from God, emphasising first that we do not think of ourselves more highly than we ought and encouraging us to use those gifts!
The Spirit of God distributes His gifts to individuals as He purposes, though we are also actively encouraged to "earnestly desire the best gifts" (see 1 Corinthians 12:31).

The call of God on our individual lives as relates to the Church of Jesus Christ is sometimes referred to as our appointment by God.

> *"And God has appointed in the church first apostles, second prophets, third teachers, then miracles, then gifts of healing, helping, administrating, and various kinds of tongues."(1 Corinthians 12:28 ESV)*

> *"And He gave some, apostles; and some, prophets; and some, evangelists; and some, pastors and teachers;" (Ephesians 4:11)*

For those who have been called into what is known as the five-fold ministry i.e. Apostles, Evangelists, Prophets, Pastors and Teachers; it appears that once they have been born-again by the Spirit of God, it is relatively easy for them to take on and run with that calling. Those for whom things do not seem as clear-cut need to spend time enquiring from God, what He wants them to do as members of His body. These would be the gifts referred to as gifts of healing, helping, administration. These have been collectively identified as the "gifts of helps" by some Bible scholars.

The period while waiting for specific direction presents a great opportunity to do with all our might, whatever our hands find to do (Ecclesiastes 9:10)!

God said to Man in Genesis 1:28:

> *"Be fruitful, and multiply, and replenish the earth, and subdue it: and have dominion over the fish of the sea, and over the fowl of the air, and over every living thing that moveth upon the earth."*

God created man with the intention that we should dominate everything (apart from other men) that He created. Even now, the Bible tells us that the whole of creation is groaning and waiting for the manifestation of the sonship in us. (Romans

8:19) His intention was that mankind, under His leadership would be co creators with Him; rising up to accomplish the mandate of leadership He has called us unto.

Leadership is a God-ordained position for everyone who yields to the prompting and leading of His Spirit. Some may resist this statement because of the abuse of leadership they may have previously experienced. Nevertheless, though not everyone leads from a visible platform, we all have the potential to be leaders once we identify our own areas of God-given strength. There is a particular role that we are meant to fill, which God, in His wisdom has already gifted us for.

We are of the seed of Abraham (spiritually) and therefore heirs according to God's promise. (Galatians 3:29)

The next verse in the fourth chapter of the book of Galatians, expounds further on this:

> *"Now I say that the heir, as long as he is a child, differeth nothing from a servant, though he be lord of all;"(Galatians 4:1)*

Therefore, for as long as we choose to be content to stay as a child and not grow into the leadership role that God ordained for us, we will remain followers and not fulfill the assignment God has for us! This is a sobering thought, particularly when we realise how much is dependent upon our choice to grow in God or to stagnate and remain stunted! It is equally important to acknowledge that the Holy Spirit places those gifts within us according to His discretion – see 1 Corinthians 12:11.

God gives the gifts according to His purpose and His divine plan and then makes a demand on what He has gifted us with. It is our responsibility to find out the specifics of what He wants us to do with those gifts. Someone with a widely celebrated gift as an orator may not necessarily be called to be a preacher, and the one gifted with a beautiful sonorous voice is not necessarily called to be a worship leader. There are so many different areas for the deployment of our God-given gifts, such that if we would only take the time to wait on Him, allowing His Holy Spirit to lead and guide us, then we surely will find ourselves walking in the centre of His will.

There is an erroneous idea which has been plaguing the Body of Christ in general. This is the idea that we are meant to be the "light of the Church"! No one actually says it that way, but our actions seem to promote this idea. In some Churches, people often end up vying for opportunities to "lead from the pulpit", or to lead some department in the Church. Conversely those who may not have easily recognisable gifts sit down and privately nurse their despair at not having discovered their own gifts!

Jesus said; "Ye are the light of the world, a city that is set on a hill cannot be hid!" He also called us the "Salt of the Earth" and we ought to realise that as members of the body of Christ, our main sphere of influence should be out there in the world – beyond the walls of our Church buildings. We all need to be aware that the plenteous harvest to which Jesus referred is out there in the secular systems and not necessarily in our Churches! May the Lord God open our eyes to the fact that you and I are the labourers that Jesus asked us to pray to God for!

Of course, the five-fold ministry mentioned earlier was put in place by God mainly for the Body of Christ; for the equipping of His saints, but it is not so that we can sit down comfortably in our Church buildings. It is so that we can be relevant in the world in which we live! We meet as believers to sharpen each other, encourage, build each other up; but this is so that we can go back to our daily lives, thoroughly equipped to bring solutions to the challenges before us.

Discovering the God-ordained purpose for our individual lives and running with that purpose does not preclude us from applying ourselves fully to "whatsoever our hands finds to do" (Ecclesiastes 9:10, Colossians 3:23). Therefore, while waiting for the purposes of God to become clear to us, it is imperative for us to find something to do. Something that God can use, in order to bless us and to make us a blessing – just like He asked Moses in Exodus 4:2; "And the Lord said unto Him, What is that in thine hand?"

Sometimes we identify a need that we are able to meet, albeit for a season. If this is the case, then let us do it with all our hearts; as serving God and not man. Many have discovered their God-ordained purpose this way.

The sheer visibility and the satisfaction of being acknowledged is a great lure for many into the music ministry, especially in these days of instant fame and viral videos. It would be foolhardy not to admit that there is something about being in that "exalted" position of worship leader or musician that is particularly satisfactory to the flesh! It is absolutely crucial for us to ensure that we are drawn by God's purpose, rather than the potential to be seen and admired by men!

Some Bible scholars have concluded that this same thing caused the downfall of Lucifer. He was gifted by God, but allowed his gifting to rule him. Satan was most likely in an exalted position among the angels in heaven as a direct consequence of his gift. It appears that he then became drunk on his own self-importance, to the extent that he decided to not only compete with God Himself, but he sowed discord amongst the angels (which God hates – see Proverbs 6:19) and there was a war in Heaven! In view of this history, everyone to whom God has given such public gifts should do all they can to guard their hearts diligently against that spirit of pride.

The Motivation:

Our motivation in the dissemination of our gifts must always come from a heart that seeks to worship God, rather than one that seeks to gain the approval, respect and ultimately the adulation of those who are being "led".

This principle, by the way, applies, not to worship leaders and musicians alone but generally in the context of Christian endeavour. It also applies to leaders within any sphere.

We all need to be students of God's Word. He knows the kind of temptations we would face so He encourages us to pay attention to His Word. If we look into His word, we can allow it to judge our motivations as it is '...a discerner of thoughts and intents of the heart'. Are we looking to glorify God or to give some attention to ourselves?

The illustration Jesus gave in Matthew 6:5 is of relevance here. Though He was speaking specifically about prayer, the principle remains the same:

> *"And when you pray, you must not be like the hypocrites. For they love to pray standing in the synagogues and at the street corners, that they may be seen by others. Truly, I say to you, they have received their reward." (ESV)*

I am absolutely convinced that neither the activity they were engaged in (they were praying), nor the location (synagogues and street corners) was the problem. The major issue was the motivation of their hearts! They did what they did "that they may be seen." Jesus says those "hypocrites" have their reward already; the fact that they have been seen! Most people would agree that this is a poor substitute as far as rewards go, for what God has prepared for those who love Him. Of what eternal benefit is the adulation of a few or even thousands of "fans", compared to the "exceeding great and precious promises" that God has given to us? (See 2 Peter 1:4). A close look at the lives of too many of those who are "idolised" in different spheres of society (but especially in the music/entertainment industry) may make one begin to reconsider the apparent desirability of the lifestyle of these "idols".

We have previously acknowledged that we do not engage in praising or worshipping God because of some rewards we are hoping to gain, instead, we praise and worship Him because He is worthy to receive our adoration! He is after all the One who spoke everything into existence and is still upholding all things by the Word of His power!

Everyone who believes that they have been called by God into the specific ministry (service) of worship and praise, must consistently through studying the scriptures, prayer, and by the Holy Spirit's power, ensure that they judge their motivations.

As we began to explore earlier, there is no doubt that the enemy has a particular strategy for obtaining the minds of men through the use of the medium of music. Therefore, it should come as no surprise that Satan is very interested in what music is like. Please note that the devil does not create anything, all he does is to pervert what has already been created by God. This is why Jesus would say of the devil "the thief cometh not but for to steal, to kill and to destroy: I am come that they might have life, and that they might have it more abundantly" (John 10:10)

Why are pop stars, actors, musicians and so many other famous people in the entertainment industry idolised today? Many are unable live out their daily lives without being under the constant scrutiny of their "adoring" public. The reward of the adoration these stars receive from their swooning fans is apparently payment enough for the lack of restraint these same fans show when invading their idols' privacy.

Unfortunately, there can be an equal tendency for us to focus our attention on those particularly gifted worship leaders or musicians leading worship in our Churches. We can easily be tempted to concentrate so much on the skill of those leading that we forget to participate ourselves. There has, in recent times, for example, been a rise of "Praise and Worship Superstars" whose attendance at a meeting, when adequately publicised is almost guaranteed, no, actually designed to pull in the crowds. There has also been a rise of the phenomenon called "Praise and Worship Concerts" where Christians are encouraged to come and have a "great time" praising God. This is not to suggest that these types of meetings are intrinsically wrong, the problem is more to do with the intents and motivations of all involved. Moreover, I have a theory that says that a lot of these so-called "superstars" may not necessarily have been called to lead worship within the body of Christ, but were rather originally called to take those gifts into the secular entertainment industry and shine the light of Jesus into the world. Some of these individuals could possibly have been in that sphere of greater influence, which by the way, is in dire need of the salt and light of which Jesus spoke; not to join the world in its perversions, but to display the multifaceted wisdom of God in a dark and dejected world. There are Christian artists bridging that larger sphere of influence as they produce material which, though may not be overtly Christian in the message, nevertheless retains the Christian principles of clean, true, positive messages in an increasingly despondent and depressed world. These materials have been produced to a high standard and is recognised and even sought after by the secular world, giving those artists opportunities to shine God's light into an area of desperate need. I have read of a Christian actor in Hollywood for example, he does not compromise his faith, but understands that God placed him in that space to be salt and light to others in that sphere.

It would be unfair not to mention the castigation that Christian artistes have been put through in the past for supposedly "selling out" by venturing into the world of secular music. Many of these artistes were persecuted (unfortunately by other Christians) for singing songs that were not overtly Christian in the content or for not mentioning the name of Jesus in their songs often enough! These Christian artists should rather be encouraged instead of discouraged, especially by lifting them up in prayer that God may grant them the boldness to stand for His Name in all they do and that they may be true ambassadors of Christ in what is essentially their workplace!

Why do we come together to praise God? What is the true motivation for instance, of the Pastor who knowingly recruits non-Christians as "temple musicians"? Is it more important that we produce music that is perfect – in terms of vocal ability, musicianship, song melodies etc., or is it equally, or even more important that those involved in leading others in true worship are themselves submitted to the authority of the One we claim to worship? Please note that this is not an "either or" situation, as I am neither advocating nor encouraging mediocrity in the Church. However, the pursuit of excellence without giving due consideration to the motivations of those we are placing in these critical positions means that we risk losing the glory of God and substituting His glory for emotional highs which do not carry the burden removing, yoke destroying anointing of the Holy Spirit!

Taking this thought further, we ought to ask; is there a place for "entertainment" in the body of Christ? A good friend recently asked me; "why don't we have Christian nightclubs"? As this is a concept I had never considered before then, I was taken aback for a moment. Having had some time to consider this and in light of my understanding of scriptures, I cannot help but conclude that there is no need for such an offering for Christians.

The scriptures are full of many verses which encourage the Christian to "walk in the Spirit"; "be filled with the Spirit" while discouraging any attempt to cater to the flesh. For example we read:

> *"Those who live according to the flesh set their minds on the things of the flesh, but those who live according to the Spirit set their minds on the things of the Spirit. For to set the mind on the flesh is death, but to set the mind on the Spirit is life and peace". (Romans 8:5, 6 ESV)*

The preceding verses leave no question as to what we as children of God should be setting our minds after. In reality, is there anyone who would knowingly trade life and peace for certain death?

A comedy of errors:

A growing phenomenon in the Body of Christ today involves incorporating actual comedy acts within Church services. Some have even gone as far as bringing in non-Christian comedians complete with their risqué "jokes" and thinly veiled innuendos. All things are lawful but not all things are expedient. The fact that the Son of God has set us free does not mean that we should once again deliberately bind ourselves to the yoke of slavery!

Entertainment is loosely defined as "the action of providing or being provided with amusement or enjoyment". As with most things for a Christian, moderation is key (Philippians 4:5). It is difficult to conclude that there is anything intrinsically wrong with entertainment; as long as it is clean, (i.e. it passes the test of Philippians 4:8 which means that it is true, honest, just, pure, lovely, of good report etc).

The scriptures tell us God is the One "who giveth us richly all things to enjoy"; see 1 Timothy 6:17. We have previously established that Jesus Christ was made manifest that we may live our lives to the full!

Somewhere at the back of my mind though, I cannot help but remember the phrase "...as it is written, the people sat down to eat and drink, and rose up to play". This was a statement made by the apostle Paul in 1 Corinthians 10:7 which was itself a direct quote from the book of Exodus 32:6; an account of the time when the children of Israel, tired of waiting for Moses to come back from the mountain, persuaded Aaron to make them a golden calf so they could worship it!

Exploring this further, the preceding verse in 1 Corinthians 10:6 declares:
"Now these things were for our examples, to the intent we should not lust after evil things as they also lusted."
This explains what the children of Israel were guilty of in the wilderness; they lusted after evil things. They began innocently enough; with eating and drinking, before rising up to play and things then degenerated into full-blown idol worship! A close look at the "evidence" tells us that they were preoccupied with satisfying their flesh.

> *"If ye then be risen with Christ, seek those things which are above, where Christ sitteth on the right hand of God. Set your affection on things above, not on things on the Earth. For ye are dead, and your life is hid with Christ in God." (Colossians 3:1, 2)*

I emphasise once again that I am not advocating mediocrity in the Church but will also hasten to add that the current trend of actively courting the opinions of the "unchurched" in order to ascertain what they think would make them consider darkening the doorway of a Church building is a slippery slope at the very least! This forms the basis of the "seeker-friendly" approach to Church growth which has undoubtedly produced a new wave of Mega Churches in recent times. The concept involves reaching out to those who are yet to be saved by making their Church experience as comfortable, non-threatening and inviting to them as possible. This of course then means the parts of scriptures which appear to be confrontational are avoided while retaining only those parts which favour the hearer.
Even in our times of congregational worship, our motivation appears to be more about producing and using those songs which (we think) compete rather favourably with the headline pop sensations of the day instead of considering whether those songs are communicating the truth of who God is, what He has

done, His promises, His ways. There is a real danger that we can get so preoccupied with attracting non-Christians to the message of the gospel (by any means necessary) that we fail to notice that we have, in reality, changed the true message of the gospel to suit the hearers.

We should remember that this is a sign of the age we live in today. These are the times predicted in the scriptures "...For the time is coming when people will not endure sound teaching, but having itching ears they will accumulate for themselves teachers to suit their own passions" (2 Timothy 4:3). The message never changes; what we may need to change is the way it is presented to different people groups. Even the apostle Paul said "…I have become all things to all people that by all means I might save some." (1 Corinthians 9:22b). Anyone who is a student of global trends in the body of Christ would agree that so many are giving in to the pressure to change the message of Jesus Christ in a bid to entice the hearers! If you were to ask yourself for example, "when was the last time I heard a message of the impending judgement of the world by God?" your own response might be telling. Moreover, you could also ask; "what proportion of messages that challenge me to grow in God, to work out my own salvation with fear and trembling, to commit to living a life that is first pleasing to God, have I heard recently; in contrast to the number of messages that I hear continually about God's love, how much He loves me, how much He wants to bless me?"

There would be no need to ask questions of this nature if you are blessed to be part of a Church family that preaches a balanced gospel, you are an ardent student of the word of God and you have learnt that the fivefold ministry (Pastors, Teachers, Evangelists, Apostles and Prophets as outlined in Ephesians 4:11) is "for the perfecting of the saints, for the work of the ministry, for the edifying of the body of Christ" – verse 12. As a result, you make good use of twenty-first century technologies and resources which allow you to access the full counsel of God irrespective of the limitations of the particular Church family to which you belong. There is no denying the fact that God loves us and wants, and indeed has, blessed us. Concentrating on these aspects of the message of the cross alone gives as much a skewed version of the gospel as does laying too much emphasis on the wrath of God and His impending judgement!

A new wave of doctrine:

In recent times, a new wave of doctrine has emerged as far as "worship" is concerned. The disconcerting thing about this new wave is the ease with which true believers appear to be getting enticed by the simplicity with which it is presented. Modes of "worship" which are not found in the scriptures at all; at least not in reference to the Almighty God, are not only being touted, but are being embraced without question. New converts to Christianity who have not had the opportunity to get grounded in the true word of God are being targeted! Practices which have origins in transcendental meditation and mystical backgrounds are being subtly added though surprisingly few people seem to be aware that this is happening. Of those that do recognise what is happening, few are taking a stand against these practices!

In the name of having unique worship experiences for example, ritualistic burning of candles and incense are being introduced. Prayer stations complete with religious props and artefacts are also rapidly gaining popularity. Although these religious props seem innocent, they could undermine the simplicity with which the scriptures encourage us to relate with our heavenly Father. We pray, knowing that He hears us; He is with us wherever we are. It is a good thing to be able to set apart some time or even some place where we consciously separate ourselves to, so we may talk to God. However, creating "shrines" for this purpose is not only unnecessary, but could actually lead to idolatry; when we begin to ascribe mystical properties to those props!

Some people are going as far as to draw physical patterns on the floor or go round "prayer labyrinths" in order to pray more effectively! Some who profess Christianity gather together in order to listen to instrumental music (known as "trance music") so they can engage in what is called "soaking". All these newly embraced practices (particularly in mainstream Evangelical, Charismatic movements) supposedly add to the "worship experience". People are seeking to "feel the presence of God" but are unwittingly opening themselves to the real possibility of demonic influences! The mere fact that worship is being promoted as something we "experience" (that is, something which happens to us) is telling enough. True worship is not something we can be passive about. True worship is active, even when we are listening for the voice of the Holy Spirit to communicate the mind of God to us. Just as Christian meditation involves voluntary (active) lip movement rather than emptying our minds. The word translated "meditate" in the Bible means to mutter, to utter, as in: "thou shalt *meditate* on it day and night…" Joshua 1:8). This new wave of doctrine suggests that the Christian "empty his mind", quieten his thoughts and just "soak" in the presence of God! Sure enough, people may "feel" something while engaging in these practices; however, we are called to a life of faith, not one where we depend on our feelings! The truth is that our feelings cannot be trusted! We have got to be vigilant! The scriptures warn us in this way: " Be not wise in thine own eyes: fear the LORD, and depart from evil." (Proverbs 3:7); and again, to test every spirit and hold fast to that which is good. There is little doubt that those who engage in these practices gain some form of an emotional high from it, but what is the eternal value of what has been gained here? For some reason, human beings seem to keep seeking ways to complicate what God has made simple! Jesus says, "If you abide in me, and my words abide in you, ask whatever you wish, and it will be done for you." (John 15:7 ESV) This does not seem to be enough though; as some people feel the need to complicate things by burning incense so that their prayers may ascend high, or lie down someplace cosy and listen to "calming" music so that they can quiet their minds in order to feel the presence of God!!!

We make it all too easy for the enemy to deceive us when we do not take the time to find out for ourselves what the scriptures say. Christians are being deceived into getting into mysticism in their bid to have a spectacular experience of worship!

There is a marked difference between congregational worship inspired by the Holy Spirit and congregational worship which is performance-based. These differences, though as divergent as night is from day, are not actually as easy to perceive as one would imagine. "Flesh minded" or carnally minded individuals would impose a requirement for an emotional high before they can conclude that a worship service has been "anointed", while those who are spiritually minded would evaluate the same time of congregational worship in terms of an inward conviction, based on faith in God's promises.

The apostle Paul writes in 1 Corinthians 2:4:

"And my speech and my preaching was not with enticing words of man's wisdom, but in demonstration of the Spirit and of power"

There is a God-ordained standard to work towards; so that even the message in our music will demonstrate the Holy Spirit and His power. Power to heal, power to deliver, power to save! Great performances which only entice the flesh or pull on our emotional strings should be left to secular concerts and should definitely not be the goal of any prescribed time of worship which is supposed to be directed towards our great and mighty God.

A cautionary tale may be appropriate here though, just in case we are tempted to swing in the opposite direction and we feel compelled to judge those we deem to be overly enthusiastic in their expressions of worship. That judgement should be left to our heavenly Father who knows the hearts of men. Let us remember David and Michal his first wife, Saul's daughter. 2 Samuel 6:16 records – "And as the ark of the LORD came into the city of David, Michal, Saul's daughter looked through a window and saw king David leaping and dancing before the LORD: and she despised him in her heart".

All Michal could see were David's physical actions; she could not tell what motivated him to act in such a scandalous way! His actions had become indistinguishable from the actions of those considered to be "worthless" persons! As Michal challenged David for his "abhorrent behaviour", he responded by asserting that he would do even worse in her estimation – "and I will yet be more vile than thus, and will be base in my own sight, and of the maidservants which thou hast spoken of, of them shall I be had in honour." (2 Samuel 6:22)

As a direct consequence of Michal's actions, she came under judgement, the Bible recording that she had no children until she died!

Our praise is to God and for Him primarily, though He wants us to declare His praise, making His deeds known amongst the peoples of the Earth. It should come as no surprise that although there will always be some who would be inspired by our praise, there will be those who not only will not be inspired, but would actively seek to discourage us.

Our time of praise is however not the time for us to "curb our enthusiasm", because, as long as our hearts are toward God, rather than in a place where we just want to be seen by men; we are sure that our praise ascends to our Heavenly Father as a sweet smelling aroma.

POINTS TO PONDER

1. Do you agree with the notion that everyone on earth has a divine call from God on their lives? Have you considered what that call is in your own life?
2. Sometimes, our true motives are shielded even from us, but the Bible is called "the perfect law of liberty" into which we can look and receive insight into our own hearts. Have you ever caught yourself just in time from pursuing a desirable thing with the wrong motives? Why do you want to be the best musician (or whatever it is you are striving for)? To glorify God or to elevate yourself?
3. What do you think about including unbelievers as musicians in a Church/worship band? What are the motives for doing this?
4. Have you come across any of the new wave doctrines mentioned? Do you think there is anything right or wrong with them? Prayer labyrinths, prayer circles, incense burning etc? Do these physical props truly and scripturally enhance worship?
5. Do we need Christian entertainment in Church? If you think so, why and how?

CHAPTER 8:

Delight yourself in the Lord.

"Delight yourself in the LORD, and He will give you the desires of your heart." (Psalm 37:4)

In both in the Old and also in the New Testaments, the same message is repeated: "praise ye the Lord", "Rejoice in the Lord", "delight yourself in the Lord", "rejoice always", "the joy of the Lord is my strength" and so much more! The message is clear; this Kingdom of God deals largely in the currency of JOY! Romans 14:17 sums it up by saying; "the kingdom of God is not meat and drink; but righteousness and peace and *joy in the Holy Ghost*."

There is no getting around this; once we have been adopted into the family of God, and have become a part of His kingdom, joy should become an integral part of our lives! Please note that joy differs from happiness. Happiness is based on the circumstances around us while joy is a gift from God and comes from within. Joy is a fruit of the Spirit – fruit that should be produced in the life of a Spirit-filled child of God. (See Galatians 5:22) We produce the fruit of the Spirit when we choose to live our lives based on the leading of the Holy Spirit, who guides us primarily through the written word; the Bible.

It is possible to look at events going on around the world today; poverty, disease, wars, terrors, perversions, etc. and erroneously conclude that there is no room for joy in a Christian's life. This is an unfortunate and inaccurate conclusion to arrive at, especially when viewed in the light of God's Word. We are in the world but do not belong to it anymore. We now belong to God and should consequently operate in a system that differs from the worldly system. Moreover, the eventual outcome has been revealed in the scriptures. God's saving grace, assures us that Christ has won – therefore we, being joint heirs with Him are also victorious! The kingdoms of this world shall eventually become the kingdoms of our Lord and of His Christ. Therefore we should stop looking at those contrary circumstances and look instead to God who has promised to keep us in perfect peace as we keep our minds on Him. When we are able to stay our minds on His promises, His love and faithfulness, we find that joy begins to well up from within us! Hallelujah!

There is a marked difference between the Kingdom of God and the kingdoms of this world. This is clearly seen in the way the two kingdom types are diametrically opposed in their different philosophies!

"But God hath chosen the foolish things of the world to confound the wise; and God hath chosen the weak things of the world to confound the things that are mighty" (1 Corinthians 1:27)

This is our God, the Almighty One, who decides to do things the way He chooses! So He says: "I will destroy the wisdom of the wise and will bring to nothing the understanding of the prudent." (1 Corinthians 1:19) and again; "...the foolishness of God is wiser than men; and the weakness of God is stronger than men". (Verse 25)

This is why God would choose to send His only begotten Son as a baby in a manger, rather than a victorious Emperor; or why our Lord Jesus would ride triumphantly into Jerusalem on a donkey, when He could have commandeered the best chariots of the land. What therefore appears as unintelligent behaviour to those who are yet to receive God's saving grace, is actually God's wisdom being manifested. By what some perceive to be mindless, God is establishing His everlasting Kingdom, using the "foolishness of preaching" for example, to save those who believe from the wrath to come!

Worldly wisdom says, "do not count your chickens before they are hatched" whereas Godly wisdom tells you first to delight yourself in God (celebrate before you actually see the results you are hoping for,) and then, He will give you what you desire. The wisdom of this world though appearing wise is actually foolish when viewed with eternity in mind, while obedience to God's instructions would often seem like a very foolish option indeed! Imagine how ridiculous the children of Israel would have looked to the people of Jericho as the marched around their fortified city!

God wants us to trust Him explicitly, leaving no room for contradiction, so that our trust leads us to obey Him, regardless of how incredulous His commands may seem to be from the natural standpoint. In the New Covenant, we are told that we "have the mind of Christ" (1 Corinthians 2:16). This should come as no surprise if we truly have Him dwelling inside us. Therefore, we have access to God's ways which even Moses could only dream about.

The key is that we have access; the choice and responsibility to find out the mind of God regarding any situation we face still rests solely on us. As the scripture says: "It is the glory of God to conceal a thing: but the honour of kings is to search out a matter." (Proverbs 25:2)

If we agree that we trust God completely, what then are those things which prevent obedience to the scriptural command to delight in the Lord?

The age of "Entitlement":

Few Christians would argue with the notion that we are living in what the Scriptures call "the last days". These are the times just prior to the return of Jesus Christ to the Earth in His glory. These are the days when men's hearts are failing them for fear; perilous times indeed! The Bible states categorically that in the last days, men shall become "lovers of self, rather than lovers of God"!

We live at a time when more people want to know: "what is in it for me?" rather than "what can I do to help someone else, even without the hope of a reward! Many are quick to announce their own good deeds while they remain skilled at apportioning blame to others for things that are not so great. In order words, while people are becoming increasingly adept at celebrating and congratulating themselves for things they have done well, they are even quicker at abdicating all responsibility for anything that fails to hit the mark, blaming anything and anyone instead. We live in the age of "do whatever makes you happy", "do what is right for you", and, "as long as you are happy and it doesn't hurt anyone else; you can do whatever you wish"! This is the age of "self" and "selfies"; the times when we are encouraged to "become a brand" in order to stand out from the rest. This is the age of the "Millennial" – that demographic cohort typically born between the early 1980s and early 2000s. Much has been said of this group who have been tagged the Me, Me, Me generation.

Mankind in the twenty first century is being sucked into the promotion and glorification of "self" with alarming speed and lack of restraint, and this phenomenon often comes with devastating consequences! It is small wonder that Narcissism (the inordinate fascination with oneself, excessive self-love) has gained a great deal of traction in recent years than at any other time in history! This same potentially destructive attitude has steadily crept into the Church, as more and more are waking up to the "Me, Myself and I" revolution. The specific part of man which the Scriptures warn us to bring to subjection; the world, led, it seems, by the explosion of communications, media and digital connectivity (particularly social media) encourages us to enthrone! We live in the age of instant gratification and hardly anyone wants to wait for anything anymore. Why should a twenty first Century Christian say, for example, "...For God alone, O my soul, wait in silence, for my hope is from Him" (Psalm 62:5)? Why "wait for God" when there are many other ways to reach a desired outcome, that is, as long as you are not too bothered about the moral implications of the means of achieving it? It is difficult to appreciate God's goodness if we not only expect it, but think that we deserve it and we want it now! How easy it is to forget that in truth, there is nothing that we have now which we have not received from God; as the Scripture says:

> *"For what gives you the right to make such a judgment? What do you have that God hasn't given you? And if everything you have is from God, why boast as though it were not a gift?" (1 Corinthians 4:7)*

As long as we continue to think of ourselves as being more deserving than others, or to use the gifts which God so freely gave to us as an instrument to oppress others, our eyes are closed to the daily evidence of the benefits He gives to us. We must remember that the gifts God gives to us are not for us only, but provide a means for us to bless others! We need to realise that we are blessed by God, not because we earned it or deserved it, but because of the unmerited favour He chooses to lavish on us. If not, we will become vain in our thinking; secretly imagining that we have done enough to deserve more from God than what we currently possess and ultimately become trapped in the quagmire of dissatisfaction.

The focus is on the wrong thing:

Jesus said in Matthew 6:25 "Therefore I say unto you, take no thought for your life, what ye shall eat or what ye shall drink; nor yet for your body, what ye shall put on. Is not the life more than meat and the body more than raiment?"

Dissatisfaction often stems from focusing our affections on the wrong things. These are the things which "the Gentiles" – those who are yet to believe in Jesus Christ seek after. The world which is without hope has no other choice but to focus on the things which they can see. The explosion of the use of social media globally, coincides with the unprecedented rise in mental health disorders such as anxiety and depression, particularly in western cultures. This rise has been particularly identified in teenagers but is increasingly affecting adults too, as social media encourages people to strive for impossible standards. We are continuously bombarded with staged images of other people having such a great time, seemingly all the time! This often gives rise to feelings of inadequacy and envy which is difficult to escape from. While most would agree that mental health problems often have complex triggers; recent research studies do identify that the rise of social media connectivity and usage is definitely playing a major role in the way people view their own lives. As long as we continue to place our focus on temporary things, comparing ourselves with one another, we are setting ourselves up for failure and actively making it extremely difficult to live a life that exudes the joy of the Lord. As members of the kingdom of God, we have access to hope beyond those things we can physically see. We understand that this world is but a glimpse of what is to come. Furthermore, our trust is in the One who created us, rather than our own ability to accomplish anything.

Interestingly, there is nothing improper about those things mentioned in Matthew. 6:25 – food to eat, clothes to wear etc.

However, when we are able to quit worrying about these things but instead focus our attention on those things of eternal value, then we see God move on our behalf and as He says in verse 33, "all these things shall be added unto you."

Praise, joy, delight in God are all demonstrations of our faith in Him because we are essentially saying; regardless of what my personal circumstances are at the moment, I choose to look at what God has done for me already. I choose to delight in God, to praise Him for what He has done and worship Him for who He is. A mindset such as this brings us liberty. We are no longer perturbed by whatever contrary circumstances may come against us. We are thus able to see the goodness and the greatness of our God in every situation.

Paralysing fear:

One of the main weapons which the enemy deploys against a child of God is fear. It is small wonder then that the Bible tells us: "Fear not!" Fear blinds a man to all the good there may be in his life, as he fixates on just those things that he is afraid of. Fear can latch on to a man in order to paralyse him and stop him from moving forward in his life.

> *"And in the fourth watch of the night Jesus went unto them, walking on the sea and when the disciples saw him walking on the sea, they were troubled, saying, it is a spirit; and they cried out for fear. But straightway Jesus spake unto them, saying, be of good cheer; it is I; be not afraid. And Peter answered him and said, Lord, if it be thou; bid me come unto thee on the water. And he said, Come. And when Peter was come down out of the ship, he walked on the water, to go to Jesus. But when he saw the wind boisterous, he was afraid; and beginning to sink, he cried, saying, Lord, save me. And immediately Jesus stretched forth his hand, and caught him, and said unto him, O thou of little faith, wherefore didst thou doubt? And when they were come into the ship, the wind ceased. Then they that were in the ship came and worshipped*

> *him, saying, of a truth thou art the Son of God. (Matthew 14:25 – 33)*

Verses 29 and 30 in the passage above recounts what happened to Peter, the disciple of Jesus as he began to step out of the comfort zone that was the boat he was on, in order to walk on water. Notice that Peter had actually started to walk on water and only began to sink when he allowed himself to take his eyes of the Lord who had bid him "Come". He began to sink as he turned his attention instead to the boisterous winds around him.

As long as the enemy can get us to focus on the raging storms of this world, he will have us trapped in a web of fear. Interestingly enough, a large percentage of what we are fearful about does not actually materialise but has achieved its goal of stopping the child of God from fulfilling God's best plan for them in that situation.

One true antidote to fear is praise. In our praise, our attention is focused on the One who is all powerful and who is totally good. Praising God in the face of fearful or adverse circumstances demonstrates our faith in God.

You may have heard of the saying that goes: "if you are not depressed, then you haven't been paying attention!" The person who originally coined that phrase was probably thinking about national or international events such as wars, terrorism, poverty and hunger, as well as the general degeneration which is prevalent in society today. That saying nevertheless illustrates the difference between the way the world thinks and the way a child of God ought to think. Our attention is not meant to be focused on the perceived hopelessness of situations; rather, our attention is meant to be focused on the One who created all things. Once the focus of our attention is right, we are able to seek and get direction from Him on what He wants us to do about the degeneration we see. Obedience to His leading this way allows us to truly be the salt of the earth and the light of the world He has ordained us to be. Rather than join the world in its depression, we are meant to shine the light of God into those situations and cause a turnaround for His glory!

We cannot give what we do not possess, and if we are just as "without hope" as the world around us, how could we ever expect to effect meaningful or lasting change?

Making melody in your heart:

"Speaking to yourselves in psalms and hymns and spiritual songs, singing and making melody in your heart to the Lord..." Ephesians 5:19

While it may not always be possible for a child of God to be happy all the time, God does expect us to lead joyful lives. We have hope for a great future in God; therefore even in the face of contrary circumstances, we are assured of ultimate victory. We have the "cheat sheet" and therefore do not have to be troubled in the same way as those people who are without hope. It is true that we are involved in a battle; nevertheless, we have the advantage of knowing that we are on the winning side. The skirmishes which we contend with while we are here on Earth are sent by the enemy in order to distract us. Instead of distracting us, they should actually remind us that we are members of the Lord's army and that "he that will live godly in Christ Jesus *shall*, (it is not optional) suffer persecution."(2 Timothy 3:12). Those battles and persecutions (which come for the word's sake) come to test the Word in our hearts. Though the enemy means for those things to stop or at the very least slow us down, we can choose to see them as opportunities for God to "show Himself strong" on our behalf (see 2 Chronicles 16:9). An opportunity for us to grow in Him and to be able to comfort others coming behind us with the same comfort that we have learnt to receive from Him.

Another reason we are told to *speak to one another* in psalms and hymns is so that we can encourage one another. In encouraging others, we find encouragement for ourselves. God never intended for us to live as "independent Christians". He planned things so that we need each other. "Iron sharpens iron, and one man sharpens another" (Proverbs 17:17). The gifts of the Spirit are distributed severally so that *all* may profit. We are only able to receive part of this profiting when we do not allow the enemy to isolate us from the body of Christ.

This voluntary isolation appears to be on the increase in these last days as more and more people become disenchanted by what they see as the betrayal of their trust, often by Christian leaders they had previously looked up to. It is easy to look on such unfavourable encounters and conclude that the best thing to do is to stop going to any Church. We may conclude; "well, God is with me in my home, I don't need to go to Church or seek the company of other believers". This is a trap of the devil! The devil will try to isolate believers in order to destroy their hope of salvation! (I sometimes wonder what would have happened in the Garden of Eden if Adam had been with his wife when the serpent came to tempt her).

We must remember that we find fullness of joy in the presence of the Lord and at His right hand are pleasures for evermore (Psalm 16:11). This is more than enough reason for us to cultivate the habit of staying in His presence, worshipping and praising Him for who He is. Let us learn to "quench the fiery darts of the wicked" (Ephesians 6: 16) as we meditate on God's Word. One of the tools for such meditation is to sing faith-filled songs... singing and making melody in our hearts unto God, instead of spending countless hours worrying and allowing contrary thoughts to rule us! We are encouraged to run the race that has been set before us with patience, fixing our eyes on Jesus who is the founder and perfecter of our faith. We are also encouraged to place our current "struggles" in the correct perspective, remembering that in our struggle against sin, we have not yet resisted to the point of shedding our own blood! (See Hebrews 12: 4)

We conclude by rejoicing in God's promise to His people, from which we can draw great hope:

> *"Sing aloud, O daughter of Zion; shout, O Israel! Rejoice and exult with all your heart, O daughter of Jerusalem! The LORD has taken away the judgments against you; He has cleared away your enemies. The King of Israel, the LORD, is in your midst; you shall never again fear evil. On that day it shall be said to Jerusalem: "Fear not, O Zion; let not your hands grow weak. The LORD your God is in your midst, a mighty one who will save; He will rejoice over you with gladness; He will quiet you by His love; He will exult over you with loud singing.". (Zephaniah 3:14 - 17 ESV - emphasis mine)*

God is in the midst of His people! He rejoices over us! He rejoices over ***us*** with loud singing! Did you see that? God sings! As much as He encourages us to sing; and we learn that His angels sing; now we see that He sings too! Those verses in the book of Zephaniah additionally give a truly beautiful picture of the fellowship Our God desires to have with us! He quiets us by His love; He rejoices over us with gladness!

We were created to bring Glory to God; we were created to fellowship with Him, our fellowship with God should cause us to worship Him because of who He is – Creator, God, and King. May we always choose to lead lives that bring glory to His Name – a chosen generation, a holy nation, a royal priesthood! A people called to *show forth* His praise and His Power!

May our lives praise You, LORD. Amen.

FINAL POINTS TO PONDER

1. Can you tell the differences between joy and happiness? Do you know what it is to experience each of these?
2. Do you agree that human beings are generally becoming more and more self serving or do you think this has always been the case?
3. Even after becoming a Christian, have you caught yourself being self serving in the guise of helping others? For example, only helping those you know for a fact would be in a position to help you in return?
4. Do you think you deserve God's favour? Since you have been good and have helped the poor, visited the sick, paid your tithes, fasted and prayed etc.?
5. Have you learnt to keep your focus on God at all times? In truth, this is not an easy thing to do, so what are some strategies you have developed to combat distractions?
6. Would you commit to keep in constant fellowship with God from now on? Opting to seek for reasons to praise Him and purposefully develop a heart of gratitude? How do you propose to go about this?

Bibliography

Sorge, B., Published April 1st 1987. *Exploring Worship: A Practical Guide to Praise & Worship.* s.l.:Oasis House.

You must be born again

> *'Do not marvel that I said to you, "You must be born again."'(John 3:7 ESV)*

Perhaps you stumbled upon this book and just decided to read it, or someone you hold in high regard placed it in your hands and said: "read this!" Regardless of how you came across this book, I am absolutely convinced that it was no accident.

Many are professing Christianity today because in some circles, it is actually a "trendy" thing to do! However, God has a different perspective. Jesus said to the young Jewish ruler: 'truly, truly, I say to you, unless one is born again he cannot see the kingdom of God.' (John 3:3 ESV) It is impossible to grasp the essence of Christian living without Christ; a "regular" human being cannot understand the principles of God's kingdom – it all seems foolish to him!

Contrary to what most people believe, the world we live in today is NOT under God's control! The first man, Adam, handed over the 'title deeds' to Satan at the dawn of time, when he chose to disobey the express will of God and chose to do his own thing instead. The chaos, brokenness, sickness and poverty prevalent in society today all give evidence to the fact that the devil is in temporary control of the world today!

The good news though, is that God has not left us to our own devices, but even before Adam sinned, He had already prepared His plan for drawing mankind back to Himself. God is Holy and cannot stand in the presence of sin; so, He sent The Sinless One; Jesus Christ His Son to take our place and receive the punishment that was meant for us (as a result of our sinful nature). Sin separates man from God, but Jesus came to bridge that great divide. He suffered greatly so that we might receive freedom from the slavery of Sin!

Everybody needs salvation, whether they acknowledge this fact or not. One day, very soon, this world as we know it is going to be done away with. Each one of us will have to face our Maker. The Bible assures us that all our "righteousness" (good works, good attitudes etc.) are but "filthy rags" in the presence of the Most Holy One. God is going to judge mankind one day, and our guilt or innocence will be determined by whether we put our faith in His Son or not!

The Salvation which Jesus provides is completely free;

> *'That if you confess with your mouth the Lord Jesus and believe in your heart that God has raised Him from the dead, you will be saved. For with the heart one believes unto righteousness, and with the mouth, confession is made unto salvation'. (Romans 10:9, 10 NKJV)*

The journey into Eternal life in God is quite simple:

1. Acknowledge that you are a sinner before the God of the Universe; you need salvation, but you cannot save yourself – (no one is exempt from this; 'for all have sinned and fall short of the glory of God,' – Romans 3:23 ESV)
2. Make a conscious determination to turn away from a life of sin; that is from living life on your own terms; instead

handing over control to the One who made you and knows what is best for you.

3. Believe in your heart that Jesus Christ, God's only begotten Son, is God in the flesh, who came down to Earth to receive the punishment that you deserve so that you can receive God's mercy and Grace which you do not deserve.
4. Confess (say with your own mouth) what you truly believe in your own heart: that Jesus Christ, God's own Son, was crucified, died on a cross, rose again from the dead and has ascended into heaven.
5. Thank God for His saving grace and rejoice; you have been born again!

You will have to trust, by faith that you have been born-again; it is not a question of feelings. In all probability, you will feel nothing at all, but you can receive God's salvation by faith and then proceed to allow Him to lead you by His Spirit. You will need to find a good, Bible – believing Church, where the word of God is the final authority and, as you draw near to God, He will also draw near to you!
May I also recommend my forthcoming book:
"Faith Foundations – a journey in Eternal life" (ISBN 978-1-9164104-1-1 – Inspirations publishing 2018) which provides a scriptural and foundational introduction to the life which Jesus purchased for us on that Cross at Calvary.

29960763R00087

Printed in Poland
by Amazon Fulfillment
Poland Sp. z o.o., Wrocław